To

Leana

Four are the Gospel Makers

Jack Wingfield FRCOG

Best wishes

Jack

First published in 2004 by
Hale Press
15 Upper Hale Road
Farnham
Surrey
GU9 0NN

Tel: 01252 711795
E-mail: info@halepress.co.uk
Website: www.halepress.co.uk

A CIP catalogue record for this book is available
from the British Library.

ISBN 0 9549439 0 2

Cover design and graphics by
mark@theinternexus.com
(www.theinternexus.com)

Editor: Elizabeth Huddleston

Produced by the Short Run Book Company Ltd
Unit 1
Orpheus House
Calleva Park
Aldermaston
Berkshire
RG7 4QW

Dedication

To my wife, for her tolerance in listening to my dogmatic opinions, waiting for them to change and to the Ministry Team at All Souls, Langham Place in Central London (where I sing bass in the choir) who, over some twenty and more years, have inspired me to study the Scriptures and have succeeded in making those opinions change.

By the same author:

Growing Up Now by Jack and Angela Wingfield

Published by Lion Publishing 1992

Contents

Foreword

The New Testament is of course the foundation text for the Christian Church. In our spiritual lives we're encouraged to allow informed imagination to take us deeper into the Christian encounter with Christ which is recorded there.

Jack Wingfield takes us another step, allowing informed imagination to reflect on the named authors of the gospels. For it was this personal experience of the good news they heard which changed their lives and so became the story they have to tell. He is reminding us that it is a personal encounter with Christ which may transform our own lives and be their foundation text. His book takes us back to the gospels with a refreshed sense of personal expectation.

Michael Till

Michael Till
Dean, Winchester Cathedral

Foreword

Introduction

FOUR ARE THE GOSPEL MAKERS

I concede that my title is not strictly the verse of the old English folk song, but I have sung 'Green grow the rushes Oh!' for as long as I can remember. It was obvious that some of the verses had a scriptural association:

> Twelve for the twelve apostles
> Eleven for the eleven that went to Heaven
> and ten for the ten commandments etc.

but it was only relatively recently that it dawned on me that all the verses were scriptural, many being drawn from the Book of Revelation.

It has always been the verse 'Four for the Gospel-makers' which has held the fascination for me. They are all 'household names'. We can read what they wrote in their Gospels, but who were they? What were they like? How did they think? What drove them to record, for posterity, the occurrences in Palestine some 2000 years ago?

My four stories do not purport to be scholarly works, nor to be 'gospel truth' and they make no pretence of being commentaries on the Gospels, but they are still more 'faction' than fiction. It all could have been so, and much of the character of the writers has been drawn directly – or by implication – from the New Testament.

Inevitably, Luke features to the greatest extent: not surprisingly really, since his contribution to the New Testament is greater than that of any other writer! He also documents a fair amount of his personal involvement with Paul in the missionary journeys in Acts, and much of the information in his gospel could only have been collected from personal contact with the family and friends of Jesus, still living in Palestine.

John, in a similar way, gives away much about himself. He is 'the disciple Jesus loved' and talks from the stand-point of one who knew him 'as from of old'. He was probably one of the same family – maybe Jesus' cousin. He is a theologian, teacher and philosopher and does not even try to chronicle Jesus' life. His intention was to write, showing the humanity of Jesus, but of greater importance to show that Jesus was divine. He wrote a lot, lived longer than the other disciples – long enough to see the dawning Christianity rise and spread from its simple origins in Palestine – and his is the last of the gospels, written even after his book of Revelation.

Mark's is the shortest gospel, although the earliest one written, but he shows glimpses of himself and includes statements of fact which only he could have witnessed, since the disciples were not around at the time, or were asleep! He is referred to often in the Pauline letters and Acts.

Matthew is the most shadowy personality, giving away little of himself, but patently fits in with the character of the well-known and hated tax-collector (hated then and hated now!), but changed by knowing, and living in, the company of Jesus.

On a recent pilgrimage to Turkey, our archaeological lecturer made a very relevant observation. He said that 'it is very difficult to touch the past'. He described an incident when he had had such an experience, raising copper ingots from a ship that had gone down in about 1310 BC, off the coast of Lycia in southern Turkey. Part way through the exercise, he had suddenly felt that he was 'with the mariners who had gone down with their ship'. If I can clothe the 'bare bones' of a name with a character and personality and generate that same feeling of association between my readers and the four Evangelists, I shall have achieved my aim.

Matthew

The Tax-collector

Matthew

The Tax-collector

I am a Jew. I always have been a Jew and always will be. I shall die a Jew! Knowing Jesus hasn't changed that. After all, he was a Jew too, and remained so to the time of his death. But knowing him has altered me and my way of life. I was collecting taxes, when I first saw him. Yes, I was one of the most hated men in the district. That didn't worry me; I had money – and if you have money, you will always have 'friends', even if other members of your family shun you. There have always been taxes of some sort or another, ever since the world began. The pagans' offerings to their gods can be classed as taxes, paid to keep them 'sweet' or 'on the people's side'. Even we have to pay Temple tax! Rome demands taxes from the whole world – for the purposes of keeping law, order, justice, roads, protection or any other excuse they can come up with. Someone has to collect them and there's a good living to be made from doing so. We were expected to collect the tax and add on a percentage for ourselves – it was part of our income – but it was this that the locals resented!

I am the second son of Alphaeus and was named Levi: James is my elder brother. When I was a young lad, Father said that I would have to learn a trade, as James had done, so that I could earn a living by the use of my hands in the typical Jewish fashion. James was always Father's favourite son, did all the right things, learned his trade and at an early age he also showed nationalistic, 'anti-Rome' leanings towards the Zealot movement. I am not a practical sort of fellow; I tried carving in wood and stone, I tried leatherwork and tent-making – all a complete disaster! I am good at figures – counting. I can work out, in my head, what costs are, proportions, measurements, what the average tradesman can expect for a day's work, whatever his trade. I can also pick up languages fairly easily – I can speak and write Hebrew and Greek; Latin is necessary for a tax-collector working for Rome and Aramaic is the language I've been brought up with. But I didn't 'fit in' with Father's expectations. I was not the usual son.

Rome has two kinds of tax-collector; the Gabbai collect the statutory taxes – ground tax, poll tax and income tax, all of which are easily calculated and although the people resent paying, the dues are 'set' and they are grudgingly accepted. The other tax-collectors are the Mokhes, as I was. These are the customs officers who have a much more interesting occupation, because the scope is so varied. There is also a different principle for collecting these taxes. A large area has a central contractor appointed to it. Many may bid for this post and it is generally sold to the highest bidder. He would not be a Roman. Cicero, a Roman statesman some hundred or more years ago, listed our profession as one of those incurring the greatest ill-will. All tax collectors are hated and therefore Rome considers the occupation to be 'vulgar'. The central contractor is usually someone from a long way outside the area where he works (probably so that there is unlikely to be any favouritism), but he appoints local collectors who know the local people and those who regularly pass through the district. We know the ways of people, their skills, what they are likely to earn – and what they will try to get away with! I knew the regulars along our trade route, all the locals and what they earned – and where they spent it. Agabus was the central contractor for customs duty for our district at that time, and when I was about twenty I had the opportunity to join his team. I had just made a botch of a building job and the mason, for whom I was working at the time, was furious with me. I stormed off the site and straight into the contractor. He obviously knew about me already and capitalised on my anger. He offered to train me, I accepted, and there it was. I spent some time as an 'apprentice', but very soon learned what was required of me (it was, after all, what I was good at – figures, calculations, reports.). Agabus kept a close eye on me for a while, to ensure I was reliable, but very soon our contact was less frequent and only for official handing on of monies and reports.

My tax booth was sited on the main road out of Capernaum; this was part of the great Eastern Road to Ptolemais, which runs through Trachonitis and Ituraea, where it was Herod Philip's territory, but it became Herod Antipas' area in Galilee – just outside Capernaum. You may well wonder how Roman law applied under Herod Antipas' jurisdiction. I was, theoretically, in the employ of Herod Antipas, but he was only a vassal of Rome, so Roman taxes were collected. As a customs officer I could challenge anyone travelling along the road, whether from the east, intending to ship goods from the port of Ptolemais, or more locally from Capernaum. Mine was a frontier post and I could stop and search anyone – strip you down completely, if I thought you might be carrying any concealed, taxable goods!

It was whilst I was sitting at my desk that I met Jesus. I had often heard him teaching a group of followers nearby. He spoke well and taught with authority and all those who listened were impressed; they would still be talking about him as they walked down the road, past me, on their way home. That day, he had been teaching at the water's edge – indeed he had come across the Sea of Galilee by boat from the region of the Gadarenes, only to find a group of men waiting by the shore with a friend who was paralysed. Jesus obviously cured him, because the man walked past me in company with his friends, but the teachers of the Law had challenged Jesus and he was explaining forgiveness of sin. He was still discussing with them when he reached me. I shall never forget that day. He looked at me and said, 'Follow me'! Jews don't talk to tax collectors, unless they have to – they hate us more than anyone else does – but Jesus spoke to me in a kindly voice and expected me to respond. I don't know what it was, perhaps his voice, perhaps his personality, perhaps something of his teaching that I had overheard from time to time, but I knew I did have to respond! Whatever I had been until then, it was time to change. I got up from my seat, left a half-written report, and walked out to join him. I didn't even stop to think what Agabus was going to say. Unconsciously, as I rose, I had picked up my pen and an unused scroll – these were the badges of my trade and profession and they were to be very useful in my future life. Jesus and I talked a lot, that day. When I left him, somewhere about the twelfth hour, to go home, I knew I must arrange a party to celebrate my change of life and to introduce him to my friends. They had to meet this remarkable man! My wife and family didn't understand what had happened to me, but they knew life was going to be different ever after.

We had the most amazing feast! Jesus came with some of his followers; there were the sons of Zebedee, the sons of Jonas and the group of Zealots – Simon, Judas the son of James and Judas Iscariot – who were great friends of my brother, James. Many of my friends, who were tax collectors, and their wives were there and others who were not acceptable in polite Jewish society. Jesus accepted my friends as though they were his. He talked to all of us and we were fascinated by him and what he had to say. The only blot on the evening was the arrival of a group of Pharisees! They certainly do not approve of us – they won't even let us in to the synagogue to pray, if they can help it. They called out a couple of Jesus' disciples to ask why he was eating with 'sinners'? When he heard what was going on, Jesus told them that 'the healthy did not need a doctor' and then quoted the prophet Hosea to them, where it says, 'I desire mercy not sacrifice' and told them to go and learn what it meant! They had no answer to that and left us in peace. All in all, we really had an evening to remember – music, entertainers, excellent food and the best company we had enjoyed together in years! Jesus was fun and serious at the same time! He obviously did not condone the way many of our profession exploited the people, but he could see good in all of us and was pleased when many of my friends conceded that they had been unfair, but resolved to change their ways. He seemed to be delighted that I had accepted his invitation to join his group of followers and to establish the change in me, he decided I should change my name. Henceforward, I would be known as Matthew – the gift of God. My family accepted that all this would mean a change in our income and standard of living, but realised that somehow, because something in me was different, I would not be able to go back to collecting taxes as I had done before. During the three years I spent travelling around Galilee, Samaria and Judea with Jesus, I managed to maintain an income for my family, using my writing and translating skills, with occasional work as an amanuensis, but he taught us, his followers, to rely on support from those we taught and healed and those who were able to provide for us. God would provide for our needs in this way. I have to say, it was not easy at first: my life-style and standard of living changed dramatically and living in the expectation that 'God would provide' went against all my previous principles – but he was quite right! As time passed, I became more accustomed to the difference and my expectations changed. I learned to depend on God and the satisfaction and fulfilment of being involved with Jesus and his work cannot be explained in financial terms.

It was not long after this that my brother, James, was invited to be one of Jesus' particular disciples. He had followed Jesus, with many others, when he was teaching nearby. He had listened, learned and was impressed. As I have said, he was a friend of the three Zealots in Jesus' group and I suspected that they might have suggested to Jesus that he should join them. They would never admit it, at the time, and after I had been in close company with Jesus for a while, I realised that I had been wrong. He had no-one 'foisted' on him! He did the inviting and all of 'the Twelve', as we became known, were there because we were especially chosen by Jesus, himself.

Soon after we had become a company of twelve, we went up to Jerusalem for our first Passover together. We left Capernaum and went south, around the Sea of Galilee, through Tiberias and on along the Jordan valley towards Jericho. It was a long journey – about 80 milia[1] and it took us seven or eight days to cover the distance, but I remember even now, the time passed very quickly. Jesus was either teaching us, as we went, or he would stop whenever a crowd gathered and teach them. We stopped at villages along the way and someone was always prepared to put us up for the night, even though we were a large party.

When I was a young fellow, growing up, I went to the synagogue every Sabbath, as did the others. We were taught by the rabbis, but none taught like Jesus did. I knew the scriptures fairly well, but he brought them to life and explained them. The other rabbis taught, but deferred to the opinions of the older, more senior teachers and always seemed to be covering their tracks in case they might offend one of their seniors. Jesus taught with authority and deferred to no-one. When I was with him, he usually taught in short bursts, aiming to clarify one topic at a time, apart from the times when we were travelling together – then he would teach as long as he thought we were listening! He seemed to think that it was better to get some points home securely, rather than 'throw too much mud at the wall' at any one time.

---

[1] A milion was about 1600 yards or 1500 metres – a little less than one mile.

On one occasion, however, I know that he taught the crowd all day. It was before I joined as part of his group, but the others told me about it and repeatedly referred to it for months after. He was in Galilee and had been healing. Crowds had gathered from all around – from Jerusalem and Judea, to the other side of the Jordan, and north of Galilee. Jesus took them up a mountainside, sat down and talked from early in the morning to late in the afternoon. There is a place there, that he knew well, which is like half a bowl. The people could sit around him on the slopes, whilst he was down on the flattened area; he could talk in a normal voice and thousands could hear him easily. In my travels since, I have seen many Roman amphitheatres – massive constructions, built for the entertainment of the people – which have been fashioned to exactly the same pattern as his natural mountain theatre. Those of the twelve, who were with him at the time, speak of his 'blessed' teaching, since he started off talking of nine sorts of people who he said were 'blessed', though they would not have thought so. The meek, the poor in spirit, those who mourn and so on. He went on to talk of them being 'salt' and 'light' and then taught on Moses' commandments. It appears, from what the others say, that he seemed to cover the entire scriptures in that one day. Parables and proverbs, treasures in heaven – you name it, he covered it. He must have been tired by the end of the day but, when he came down from the mountain, he still had the strength and compassion to heal a leper and a centurion's servant. Then, on top of that, when he got to Simon Peter's home, where he was going to stay for the night, he found that Peter's mother-in-law was ill. He made her well and she prepared a meal for them. Then many more sick and demon-possessed were brought to him. He must have been completely exhausted. It is not surprising that people were still talking about that day when I joined the group.

The first time I saw his healing power in action was soon after I had joined him. He was approached by one of the synagogue rulers, whose daughter had been ill and had just died, but he was quite sure that if Jesus laid a hand on her she would live and be well. Jesus went with him, but on the way, a woman deliberately touched the fringe of his cloak. Her monthly loss had gone on for years and it was making her ill with so much loss of blood – she really should not have been out mixing with others because this loss made her ceremonially unclean. She seemed to know that contact with Jesus could make her well. Now, with all those people around him, Jesus knew she had touched him and why! We all teased him and said it was impossible to know that someone had intentionally touched him amongst all those jostling to be near him. But he did know. He sought her out from the crowd and told her she would be well, because she had faith. After this diversion, he went on to the ruler's house: he was met by the family who laughed at him when he said the girl was just sleeping, but he took the ruler's dead daughter by the hand and brought her back to life! I have to say I was impressed!

Over the years I was with Jesus, it began to dawn on me that as he taught, the scriptures not only made sense, but they applied to him! He was the King, the Holy One, the 'Son of David' they were talking about. Many things written by the prophets of old, over which he could not possibly have had any control, described him and forecast what was going to happen to him. He was fulfilling their prophecies!

Let me explain: for instance, the Prophet Nathan had told King David that his 'house' would last for ever and Isaiah had said that the Messiah would come from Jesse – King David's father. Both of Jesus' parents were of the house and lineage of King David. Also he would have been born in Nazareth, had it not been for an edict by Caesar Augustus that a census should be taken. That had meant that his mother and father had had to go to Bethlehem when she was about to go into labour – so he was born in the city where the Prophet Micah had said the Messiah would be born! Isaiah had said that the Anointed One would be 'born of a virgin' and Jesus was the first-born in his family. Jeremiah warned that 'Rachel would weep for her children' – all know that he was speaking of our nation – and, not long after Jesus was born, Herod had tried to kill him by ordering the destruction of all little boys under the age of two years.

Now there is yet more that is interesting, relating to that horrific command, which we learned one day when we were all in Capernaum and met Jesus' mother. She told us that after his birth, they had stayed in Bethlehem for some while, to allow any scandalous talk about them having a baby when they were only betrothed, to settle and grow old. One day, unexpectedly, three eastern strangers arrived with gifts 'for a king'. They were magi – astrologers, men who studied the stars. They had seen two stars – Jupiter, called the king of the gods, and Saturn, which was related to the Jews – so close to each other that they looked like one very bright star – together in the part of the night sky they called Pisces (the fish) which, they said, had an influence around Judea. They told Mary and Joseph that this meant a king of the Jews was to be born in Judea – and now they had found him! So they gave the young Jesus the precious gifts they had brought – three beautiful little caskets containing gold, frankincense and myrrh. That night, after they left, Joseph had a visitation from an angel, who told him that he had to take Mary and Jesus out of the region – and fast. There was a risk to their lives! The wise men had gone to the palace first, and had talked about the new king to Herod, who would now try to find the little family. They would be better off in the safety of Egypt. So they packed the little caskets and as many of their belongings as they could expect their donkey to carry – in addition to Mary and young Jesus – and headed out, on their own, towards Hebron, then west to reach and follow the Via Maritime southwards towards Egypt. It was the safest route for lone travellers, and away from Jerusalem, so they managed to avoid Herod's vicious destruction of the young children. They stayed in Egypt for a few years until Herod's death. Joseph's trade, as a worker with wood, was useful everywhere, so they lived fairly comfortably until they returned to Nazareth – they did not do it thinking of the scriptures, but even this fitted with Hosea's saying that the 'Holy One' would 'come out of Egypt'!

Malachi had said that a messenger' would precede the Messiah and Isaiah said there would be one crying in the desert, 'Prepare the Way of the Lord'. Just think of his cousin John the Baptiser. We had not had a prophet in our nation for more than four hundred years – until John. He was a bit older than Jesus, started his ministry before him, lived, preached and baptised in the desert, and recognised Jesus as the 'Holy One of Israel' and called him the

'Lamb of God' when he baptised him. Jesus called John the 'latter day Elijah' and knew that John was the one sent ahead of him.

Now I know Jesus certainly fulfilled one prophecy, just before he was crucified, by riding into Jerusalem on a donkey, as Zechariah had forecast more than 500 years ago. But, as I recall, Jeremiah[2] predicted that Jesus would be betrayed for 'thirty pieces of silver' and these would be given to 'the potter', which happened with Judas, one of our company, and Jesus could not have arranged that one! Even less could he have had control over his burial. There is a strange, prophetic verse in the book of Isaiah, which made no sense until Jesus was buried – it says 'he was assigned a grave with the wicked and the rich in death'. Having been crucified, Jesus was not even entitled to proper burial (the bodies of executed criminals were simply thrown on the slow burning rubbish tip to the south of the city wall), but he had a rich man's grave when Joseph of Arimathea – a member of the Sanhedrin – asked Pilate's permission to take his body for burial and laid it in a new tomb which had been cut for his family, in his own garden.

Throughout the time I was a member of the Twelve, Jesus always insisted that his principal ministry was to teach and to open up the scriptures to the Jewish nation – 'salvation' for all men would then follow via the Jews. Indeed, the first time he sent us out as a group to teach and heal, he insisted that we should not go to the Gentile towns nor Samaria – although, thinking back, that was probably because he knew that we were not sufficiently experienced to

---

[2] Matthew made an error: the prophecy was made by Zechariah cf. Chap. 11 v 12,13.

cope with other than our 'own kind'! Typically, though, when we were once in the region of Tyre and Sidon, and a Canaanite woman asked him to help her sick daughter, he told us – and her – that he was sent only to the 'lost sheep of Israel'. (She, however, knew that he could help her and persisted with her request and he healed her daughter because of her faith in him.) Jesus' problem was that despite his efforts, most of our nation would not accept that the son of a carpenter, who was not of a Pharisaical background and who had not had formal rabbinical training, could possibly be the Holy One of Israel! He was literally thrown out of the synagogue in his own home town of Nazareth, when he once read a passage from Isaiah on the Sabbath and told the congregation that 'the scripture was fulfilled that day in their hearing'. It was as a result of that episode that he never went back there again, but made his base, thereafter, in Capernaum, on the shores of Galilee. The townsfolk of Nazareth could cope with him teaching in the synagogue, but baulked at the idea of him 'fulfilling' the scriptures. But Isaiah had promised that the 'Holy One' would cast out demons, heal the sick, open the eyes of the blind and make the lame walk. I saw Jesus do all this, as Isaiah had said – and raise the dead too! I saw so many of the old scriptural prophecies fulfilled whilst we were living and travelling with him. It is so frustrating that our nation will neither see nor listen! They have learned the scriptures, but they are missing the point of them. I have tried to explain them – as Jesus taught us – whenever I have been teaching. I have put in writing all he taught, in Hebrew – their own language – so that it can be read over and over again by each of the communities of converts we have established around the country. They can then read them to their near neighbours, too. It is important that all these facts are recorded and shown to our nation!

Jesus most often taught in parables. He told the people stories of things they knew about and understood, but used them to teach the meaning of the scriptures and God's kingdom and (though somewhat obscurely), that the prophets of old were pointing towards him. He told of fishermen casting nets, sorting out the fish and throwing the bad ones away. He told of a sower casting seed and likened the hearers to the ground on which the seed fell: he told of weeds being sown in a field of grain being left until harvest, lest the grain be damaged in trying to pull them up earlier. He told them of a landowner who rented his vineyard to some farmers and in due time, sent his servants to collect his share of the fruit. The tenants beat his servants and even killed his son (as was to happen to Jesus himself), when he finally sent him to try to collect the dues. Often people would listen to a story with apparent interest, but did not understand the underlying meaning and were not sufficiently moved to ask him to explain it to them. He sometimes tried to catch their attention by being humorous, or making a story so ridiculous that they would have to laugh. How, for instance, could they ever see a loaded camel squeezing through the eye of a needle? Even during his 'blessed' teaching that I have told you about, he talked of giving cloak as well as coat to someone who was demanding it – can you imagine the average Jew stripped down to his loincloth in public? But often whatever he said still didn't help. Hadn't Isaiah prophesied of the Children of Israel, 'You will be ever hearing, but never understanding; ever seeing, but never perceiving' – and Jesus said he wanted our nation to show an interest and ask questions and then he could teach them more – but they had to show an interest, first, and they had to ask! If they didn't, he never forced the scriptures or his teaching down their throats! He certainly expected us to ask, enquire, show an interest and believe that what he said, he meant. He often seemed to be exasperated with our lack of faith and understanding, but he always patiently explained when we lacked insight. He explained that there was a great burden of responsibility placed on those who did understand – much more would be expected of them – and he was referring to us! It was a long time before we really learned to have faith. Indeed, you might even say our faith did not truly become established until the feast of Pentecost after Jesus had left us. We believed – but we didn't believe, if you know what I mean. We trusted that God would provide for our needs; we were sent out to teach about the kingdom of heaven, to heal the sick and to cast out demons – and we all believed that we could do so, and we did it! But it was more that we did it because Jesus had told us we must do so. We did it all according to his instructions and believed that if he had said it, it would all work. We didn't really have the faith – our own trust – that God would enable us to succeed. We still didn't understand.

Let me tell you a few stories to explain how slow we were to appreciate who Jesus was and to understand the message he was trying to convey. One was before he called me, when the group was crossing Galilee in Peter's boat, just after he had healed the centurion's servant. Jesus had been teaching about faith and was with them, asleep on a

pillow in the stern. A violent storm had blown up –
as it can, without warning, on Galilee. The waves
were tossing them about violently, water was coming
aboard and the disciples, baling frantically, feared
that the boat would go down and they would drown.
They could not cope with the idea that Jesus was
calmly asleep so they woke him, accusing him of not
caring whether they lived or died. 'Why are you
afraid?' he had asked them. 'After all I have told you
about faith, do you not believe that God will look
after you and keep you from drowning?' He had
then stood up in the boat, rebuked the storm and
both the wind and the waves had settled instantly!
Storms on Galilee abate as quickly as they arise – but
not the waves. They were all astonished! They had
not understood the significance of who it was that
they had in the boat with them.

The other stories relate to things that happened
towards the latter part of Jesus' ministry, much later
on (by which time we should have all known better.),
when I was there too. You will remember that John
the Baptiser's disciples had sought out Jesus to tell
him that John had been killed by Herod; he was upset
and tried to get away to be quiet for a while, but a
crowd of about five thousand followed him a long
way out of town. It was late in the evening, they
were hungry and he had fed them all with the small
amount of food a young lad had carried for himself –
five little loaves and a couple of fish! Something
similar had also happened some while later, this time
using the food we had taken for ourselves. On both
occasions Jesus had made us gather up the left-overs
and they had filled many baskets. Another time, we
were all in the boat on Galilee and the day was at
least calm. I'm no fisherman and I don't like the sea,

but the sea was flat, with just a light wind and we were sitting in the stern of the boat, looking at the breeze filling the sail and travelling smoothly across the water. Jesus began talking to us of 'the yeast of the Pharisees'. This time we thought he was complaining that we had not brought enough bread with us. He despaired! He was trying to explain to us that the Pharisees were misinterpreting the Law and their teaching was spreading – like yeast in dough – and spoiling the ordinary people's worship of God and we must be wary of it. He wasn't worried about bread! He had only just shown us that many could be fed with next to nothing, provided we had faith in God. We had not only missed the significance of his ability to feed a multitude with very little – as well as missing the point of what he was telling us – but we had shown our lack of understanding of whom he was and the meaning of faith, too!

I had never known anyone with such knowledge of the scriptures as Jesus had. He was always able to quote chapter and verse in support of any topic on which he was teaching, or to justify his point of view when challenged by the authorities – much to their irritation. It was this fact that caused much of the friction and conflict that was to lead to their pursuing him to his death. He taught about the Kingdom of God and that to be part of it was a gift from God, available to our entire nation. The Pharisees had cluttered worship with so much unnecessary ritual that it seemed almost impossible to approach God, even via the priests. He taught that we should be able to approach God as a child goes to his father – even to the extent of calling God 'Daddy'! During his 'blessed' teaching that I have already told you about, and many times since, he wanted us to use a prayer that did just that. It took bits from the Psalms, Proverbs and other familiar prayers and made a simple, concise and comprehensive prayer – but he began it with 'Daddy'! It is so different from any of the formal synagogue prayers that we call it our Lord's Prayer.

He has often told us, and others, that if we don't approach God with child-like simplicity and honesty, we just do not understand what God wants of us. He has even been known to take a child out of the crowd to demonstrate what he meant. It sounds so simple, but the implications are far-reaching and hard because, as he said, it may result in giving up wealth and position (as I know) and separating members of a family, if others cannot accept what he says. I remember an occasion when he really offended his family, by saying this. He had been teaching in the big room of a house that he often used in Capernaum, when he was told that his mother and brothers were outside, asking to speak to him. He replied that all who did the will of God were his mother and brothers, pointed to us and said we were his mother and brothers. He was not very popular with the family after that!

When we came back to Galilee for the third time (and just after the time when Jesus had fed the vast numbers of people with next to nothing, that I was just telling you about), we went on northwards to Caesarea Philippi, near the source of the Jordan, at the foot of Mount Hermon. In times gone by, when the town was called Paneas, Herod the Great had built a marble temple for Caesar Augustus there. Herod Philip – his son – changed its name to Caesarea and added his name to differentiate it from the port to the southwest. It was there that Peter actually put into words what we had all begun to think about our Master. Jesus was asking what other people were saying about him and who we thought he was. Peter said we believed he was the 'Christ', the 'Son of God'! Jesus said he did not want anyone outside our group to know this, yet, but then, strangely, he began to try to warn us that he was going to die soon. How could he be the Holy One and be going to die? We all knew that he was unpopular with the Authorities and they would have liked to have him out of the way, but how could this be if he really was the Holy One? We were going up to Jerusalem and he said that he would suffer at the hands of the Authorities, would be killed – but would then be 'raised to life on the third day'. He said that anyone who followed him must be prepared to 'take up his cross', too. We all knew what crucifixion meant! Too often we had seen the Roman punishment exacted. A man driven through the streets with scourges, with his arms tied to the heavy crossbar of his cross on his shoulders – ready to fix his arms (when he reached the place of crucifixion) with a big nail through each wrist. He would then be hauled up off the ground, hanging from the crossbar and his feet would be fixed together to the upright by another nail. Then exposed, naked and nailed, he would be left to die. Pilate, the hard and cynical Roman Governor, always arranged for three to be 'done' together – company for each other, he used to say. We couldn't understand why Jesus was talking like this. He could not possibly think that such a terrible punishment would be meted out to him; he had done nothing to justify it. But it was to happen – in just that way, too.

Jesus warned us several times, after this, that he was going to die, but that one occasion seemed to be a turning point, both in things that happened and things that he said. Everything then began to point directly to the fact that he was the 'Son of God' and the 'Expected One', as the scriptures had clearly described. (What we really did not understand then, was that each time he talked of his death, he also said that he would be 'raised to life on the third day').

It was about a week or so later, that Peter and the Zebedees (James and John) excitedly told us that they had been up a mountain, with Jesus, where the strangest thing had happened. Jesus had been standing a little way away from them when he seemed to begin to glow. His face shone and even his clothes became a brilliant white! They thought, at first, that it was a trick of the sun, but then two men appeared standing beside him. Even to the bemused three, these were patently Moses and Elijah and they spoke with Jesus. Then a mist came up and hid them, but they heard a voice saying, 'This is my son — listen to him!' When the mist cleared, Jesus was alone, looking as normal as ever. They were stunned! Jesus told them not to be afraid, but not to tell anyone about it until he had been raised from the dead. He had said it again and still didn't explain, but as they talked — coming down from the mountain — they did begin to understand that John the Baptiser was the 'Elijah' that was expected to come in advance of the Holy One of Israel, to prepare the way.

Another time, when we were at Capernaum, the collectors came for temple tax. Jesus asked whether kings collected tax from their sons. Obviously they did not, and Jesus implied that he should, similarly therefore, be exempt from temple tax. They completely missed that point, but to confound everyone, he told Peter to catch a fish, open its mouth and there would be a coin to cover his and Peter's tax. He did so, and there was a four drachma coin!

I am quite sure that the most important happening, before his death, was his entry into Jerusalem a few weeks after this. He had taught parables, he had been challenged by the authorities on his teaching and had thrown it back on them, in telling the people not to accept the teaching of the Pharisees because they did not practise what they preached. But, when he decided his time was come, he sent two of our company into Bethphagae (on the eastern side of the Mount of Olives) to borrow a donkey and her foal – he had obviously made arrangements for this in advance – and rode into Jerusalem fulfilling Zechariah's prophecy; her 'king' was coming in meekly, on a humble steed. You should have seen the crowds! They cheered, shouted 'Hosanna!', strewed palm branches in his way and nearly went mad with excitement. They knew that this was The Holy One, the prophet of the scriptures! He rode through the Susa gate up to the Temple, but there the 'temperature' changed. In the outer courts were the money-changers and sellers of animals for ritual sacrifice. Everyone knows that their rate of exchange for temple coinage – necessary for the purchase of animals for sacrifice – is illegal and that animals should not be bought and sold for such inflated prices. I had never before seen Jesus show anger, but now he was like a madman! He knotted up some thick cords, made a scourge and drove the tradesmen out, overturning the money-tables and quoting scripture from Isaiah at them, saying that his house was to be a house of prayer and they were making it a den of thieves. He left the onlookers in no doubt that he was associating himself with both the scripture and the Temple!

When all had calmed down, we went back to Bethany for the night. This was the first day of the week and we went up to Jerusalem each day, after that. Jesus taught in the Temple courts daily, healing and still teaching in parables, but the tenor of the parables had now changed. He was no longer using stories related to things the people knew – things in common use – they were now all related to him as the Holy One, the King. Each evening, we went back to Bethany; mostly we stayed with Lazarus and his sisters, but the last night we were there, we were invited to dinner at the home of Simon the leper. During the meal, whilst he was reclining at table, a woman came in, broke open a jar of exquisite, expensive perfume and poured it over Jesus' head. There was much murmuring as to why she had done it and how much money it could have raised if sold, for the poor. He instantly sprang to her defence, saying that the poor will always be around and we should always be aware of their presence and look after them, but she had done something very special for him whilst he was still with us. Indeed, did we but know it, he would be dead within a couple of days. I suppose that even when he was on the cross, that perfume would still have wafted about him. He also said that wherever the gospel was preached, this story would be told of what she had done for him in recognition of who he was and in preparation for his death – I suppose that is what I am doing, even by telling you of the story!

It must have been soon after this that Judas agreed to tell the chief priests where and when they would be able to apprehend Jesus.

On the first day of unleavened bread – and earlier than we would have expected – Jesus said that we were going to eat the Passover meal together. We went into Jerusalem, to the home of the family with whom we had often stayed, when in the city, and Jesus had obviously made arrangements to use their big room – the password was to say, 'The teacher says "my time is near"'. The room was already set up for all of us. All the symbols were prepared; there was the bowl of salt water – the tears shed in Egypt; the bitter herbs – the bitterness of slavery; the 'Charosheth paste' of dates, apples, pomegranates and nuts – the clay with which the bricks were made, with cinnamon sticks for the straw; finally, the four cups of wine – God's four promises from Exodus. Their son John Mark and servants served us throughout the evening. During the meal Jesus worried us all by saying that someone in the room was going to betray him to the authorities. We were all stunned and couldn't believe that any one of our company could even contemplate such a thing! He obviously said something to Judas during the meal because he got up and went out. What Jesus must have said, we didn't realise until much later. Judas was the keeper of the common purse, and we had assumed that he had gone out to give a donation to the poor – as was the custom of many, during the Passover meal. Little did we know what he was actually doing.

Towards the end of the meal, Jesus did something else which was strange and we did not understand what it meant. In the Jewish tradition he broke bread, but told us it represented his body and told us to eat it. Then, again in traditional fashion, he gave us a cup of wine to drink, saying it was his blood poured out for the sins of many. He told us to remember him every time we broke bread and drank wine. It was some while later – long after he had risen – that its significance dawned on us; he had been telling us that he was to be the Passover sacrifice!

After the meal was over, we went out singing, past the Pool of Siloam, through the city gate, along the Kidron valley near the city wall to Gethsemane – an olive grove, halfway up the Mount of Olives which we all knew very well. Jesus wanted to pray; he asked most of us to wait for him and, as was his custom, took Peter, James and John with him and went further up the hill. We sat amongst the trees in the cool of the night air and talked for a while. It was quiet, late, and after a meal; as time went on, we dozed a little. Then someone heard noises and we all started up! We could see the city wall quite clearly and there, coming through the Susa gate, were Temple guards with torches and others with them. We watched as they came down the slope to the Kidron brook, crossed over and started up our side of the valley. They were coming towards Gethsemane! Why? They were certainly coming our way – and on business. We got up quietly and started to move up the hill towards Peter and the others. As we did so, Jesus had come down to them and found them sleeping. As he was waking them, we reached them – but so did the guards. Then we realised where Judas had gone when he left the meal – he was leading the group of guards, priests and elders. He went up to Jesus and embraced him. Instantly, the guards arrested Jesus and we tried to get him free again. Peter had a sword and struck out, cutting off the ear of Malchus, the high priest's servant. Jesus told him to put up his sword, picked up the ear – and stuck it on again! He said that if he wanted to, he could call up twelve legions of angels to defend him – but then the scriptures would not be fulfilled. At that point the guards turned on us. We were outnumbered. We scattered, ran further up the hill towards the roads to Bethany and Jericho, not stopping to find out whether we were still being followed. When I stopped for breath, with heart pounding, there were only three of us together; where the others went we didn't know – but the guards were no longer following us! We three went on to Bethany, to the home of Lazarus, Martha and Mary, scared, worried sick, not knowing what to do, wondering what had happened to Jesus and feeling guilty for running away. What else could we have done? We were outnumbered and defenceless. We woke up Lazarus and his sisters and told them what had occurred. They put us up for the night, and we stayed with them the next day. We laid up in a barn, out of sight, as we thought that the guards might search the area for us, as troublemakers, and arrest us too. It was not until late the following day, after the Sabbath was over, that a traveller along the Bethany road told Lazarus that Jesus had not only been arrested – he had been crucified and buried too! We were distraught! We had run away from the guards, but we didn't dream that Jesus would be killed – and in such a terrible fashion. We had left him on his own – to face that! Somehow, we felt that we couldn't stay any longer in the safety of Bethany. We decided that we should leave and go back to Jerusalem, as soon as it began to get dark, to the home of Jesus' friends, where we had eaten our last meal with him. We figured that the others would probably do the same and we could then all plan what to do next. We were right. Peter, Andrew and James bar Zebedee were already there. James told us that John had been in earlier, but had gone back to their house to Mary, Jesus' mother, who was being comforted by his own mother. He didn't need to explain what state Mary was in! John could be contacted and kept in touch with what was happening, and the others would, no doubt find us too. It is difficult to describe how we felt, at that time; a mixture of fear and anger, guilt and remorse, sorrow and depression. We had let down our leader and he had been killed. We had hoped for so much: Jesus was going to change the world – and he had been simply disposed of by the authorities! We sat silently despondent for some while and then Peter spoke. He had obviously been steeling himself to say something. We had only run away, he said, but he had got into the high priest's courtyard with John, who was known by the staff because his family supplied the kitchen with fish. He was twice challenged by a couple of the servants standing around, as being a follower and had denied it. Then, a third time, his speech was recognised by a serving maid as Galilean and she was sure he was one of the followers. Peter said that he cursed and swore and vehemently denied ever having been with Jesus and then he heard a cock crow! Jesus had said it would happen, despite Peter's earlier protestations that he would never disown him and would follow him to the death, if need be. There was Peter in that room with us, a big, powerful man – now a tearful, despondent heap.

Time dragged. Little was said. No one wanted to eat nor drink. No one could sleep. We were all afraid that any voices outside the house would be officials coming to take us away too. Somehow we survived. Before early light, we did hear voices and people running and then there was the sound of someone coming into the house – but it was my brother James and Simon the Zealot. As the early shafts of morning light appeared, John returned, bringing in Judas, James' son. We were all accounted for – except for Thomas.

Then there was a great commotion – Mary of Magdala ran in breathless, up the steps to our room, banged on the door, demanding that we let her in, saying that the tomb was empty and she had seen Jesus! She and Mary, who had been with her at the crucifixion, had gone to the tomb again. They had gone early, before light, because they didn't want to meet anyone – they would be trespassing in Joseph's garden. Mary said that on the way they thought they had heard thunder and when they got to the tomb, the stone had been rolled away, the guards were nowhere in sight, the tomb was empty and there was an angel there, who told them that Jesus had risen and was going to Galilee, and they had to tell all of his disciples. Mary then said she had seen Jesus and she had run all the way to tell us. Well! What were we to say? Women! Neurotic, hysterical and now imagining that the dead could rise. To say that Mary was offended that we did not believe her is something of an understatement. She told us that we could believe what we liked, but she knew! If God wanted to do something, then anything was possible and if he wished, he could raise Jesus – even if he was dead. And hadn't Jesus himself said that he would rise again on the third day? We had said often enough – she reminded us – that we had not understood what he meant. Well now it had happened! We did think that she had one good point; it would be a good idea to go to Galilee, as far away from the authorities as we could reasonably get. And then... Jesus appeared to us! He was Jesus – but different somehow. He told us that we should go out to all the nations, teach them and baptise them and that he would always be with us.

Galilee was the same as it always was for us – quiet, familiar and, above all, safe. We were far enough away from Jerusalem to get wind of any movement of the authorities or their agents coming towards us in the north. We were all fairly sure that the high priest's agents would be after us, since he had instructed the detachment of Temple guards – who had been on duty at Joseph's tomb – to let it be known that we had stolen Jesus' body whilst they were asleep. The rumour was that the guard had been paid handsomely to say they had fallen asleep on duty and that we had come along and removed the body so that we could say 'He had risen from the dead'! We thought that we would probably have to be silenced so that their story would hold. We were amazed that they could produce such a story and even admit that the guards could have been asleep on duty! Who would believe, after all that had gone on at the time of the arrest, that we could have formulated any plan, let alone one as calculated and daring as that? We were frightened, totally disorganised and had scattered to the four corners of Jerusalem. At least, when we got back to Galilee, we all felt secure enough to be able to go out: Peter, Andrew and the Zebedees reverted to type and went out fishing – something they knew well, could do well, and which took their minds off the devastation of Passover. There they had the advantage over me; they could return to their old occupation, but there was no way I could return to mine. Even if I had wanted to do so, no-one would have given a second chance to a tax gatherer, who had walked out on his employer! I was committed to Jesus, and there it was.

Jesus appeared to us many times in and around the old, familiar places, but as Pentecost approached, he told us to be in Jerusalem for the Feast and wait for the Holy Spirit. We had no idea what he meant; what was this 'Holy Spirit'? What was it all about? He didn't explain. All we knew were the risks of being in the city. We returned with more than a few misgivings, but he appeared to us there and walked with us out to Bethany. We talked together and he told us again what we would have to do in the world. He blessed us – and then he left us – he was with us one minute and then he seemed to disappear almost literally into thin air! We were just left standing there. We didn't know what to say to each other; we stood there just looking into space, feeling just a little stupid, as though we had lost something, but not quite knowing what, nor what we ought to do about it. Someone said we ought to go back to Jerusalem, but we decided that Bethany was safer, so we did the familiar thing and went to find Mary, Martha and Lazarus. They were pleased to see us and we stayed with them for a few days – until the Feast of Pentecost. Early that morning, we all set out for the city and made for another safe house that we knew well, at the end of the Street of the Sandal Makers. We were sitting in their big room talking when the room suddenly seemed to fill with noise and fire and something happened to each of us in turn. We knew we had been filled with the Holy Spirit! Don't ask me to explain it. We all knew that something had happened to us and we had been changed. The easiest thing to describe is that as a result of whatever had occurred in that room, we were no longer fearful of the authorities; we went out into the streets to tell everyone about Jesus and what he had taught us.

Peter was terrific! We were all accused of being drunk, but he said it was far too early in the day for that, and didn't everyone there realise that they could all understand what we were saying? We were all speaking to strangers in their own languages; although I have an ability with languages, most of the others have little more than their native Aramaic and some Hebrew and there were people there from all parts of the world, especially for the Festival. They could all understand what we were saying! We were only six or seven stadia[3] from the tomb in Joseph's garden. We knew it was empty and we knew why – we were going to tell the world and we didn't care what the authorities either said or did about it!

Fired – literally – with the Holy Spirit, we spread far and wide teaching, preaching, baptising and healing as Jesus had instructed us. Jerusalem had now changed from being the place we all avoided for fear of the authorities and had become our base. For some while, we would return intermittently to meet up, exchange experiences, talk of new converts and new places. As time passed, however, we moved further afield, we met less and less frequently and I travelled south to Egypt. I have been here now for

---

[3] A stadion is about 200 yards or 185 metres

five years and there are thriving communities of believers from the Nile Delta to the Sahara and I am now planning to take my team of workers even further south towards Nubia (or 'Cush' as we know it in Hebrew). It is going to be a very long time before I can return to Jerusalem to meet up with any of the others again!

[Tradition suggests that Matthew died a martyr in Nubia (Ethiopia)]

Mark

The Young Man

Mark

The Young Man

Have you ever noticed that sons, at naming, are often given two names? Mothers frequently use both – particularly when they are cross – but again, it is interesting that family and friends tend to use one name, whilst the other is reserved as an 'official' name – for documents, writings and in other rather formal circumstances. It is the same for me: my family and friends call me John, but I sign Mark – in fact, I'm writing a letter now – Peter's teaching and his stories about Jesus – and as it is a serious discourse, I shall sign it that way – Mark! Well, Yohanan is my Jewish name, which means 'Yahweh has shown Grace', but Marcus is Latin – Roman – it sounds more official – better as a signature. It is the same with Saul Paullus, who is now well known as a leader of The Way. In Jewish circles he is still known as Saul, a Jew of a pharisaical family, but as a Roman citizen of Tarsus, his Roman name Paul carries much more weight around the world and, indeed, has been very helpful in his ministry.

My family has lived in Jerusalem for as long as I can remember. Father and Mother had always been comfortably off, as they say, and we had a nice house – big – with several rooms upstairs – a small garden and servants. One of the benefits of having an affluent family is that I was 'put to school' and learned to speak and write Latin and Greek. At the time I hated it, but now I find that both are invaluable; Greek is essential for writing to and teaching the many new converts to the faith around the world. Father died many years ago, not long after Jesus was crucified, but my mother (Mary) died just a few years ago. She was very frail in her latter years, but sharp and bright to the end – and a true believer!

Our house was always a meeting place for Jesus and the Twelve and for his other close friends, both during Jesus' lifetime and after his death and resurrection. Indeed, when Peter escaped from Herod's prison, the first place he made for was our home. A wanted man, in the dead of night, just escaped from jail and what happened? That idiot of a servant girl, Rhoda, got so excited that she ran into the main room and left him at the door. Outside! At risk! It is just as well that I was not there at the time: I would have been furious. But, as I say, ours was a house where the followers met and prayed.

I remember well the last time Jesus and the Twelve met at our home. It was the first Passover after my bar mitzvah. They used our big room, upstairs, for their Passover supper. Father had told Jesus he could have the room any time he wanted it – I don't know what Jesus had done for him, but it must have been something very special. What was fascinating, looking back on it, was the intrigue involved before the supper. Firstly, the meal was arranged a day earlier than expected and secondly, quite obviously Jesus did not want the disciples to know where they were going for supper. He had arranged a special sign with Father; a man-servant should be sent to draw water and carry the jar on his shoulder as he made his way back to the house. He was not pleased, since fetching water is the women's job! This was to be just before sun-down and he (Jesus) would tell the disciples to follow the man wherever he went; they were to ask the owner of the house where he stopped, 'Where is the room that has been prepared for us to meet?' It was, of course, our big room. I suppose it was to stop anybody disturbing their meal: if the authorities had known, he could even have been arrested at my home!

In those days, as a young fellow, I was very inquisitive – perhaps I still am. I wanted to know what was going on, but I was only allowed into the big room to carry in dishes of food and a wineskin. Mother kept a close watch over me to be sure I didn't stay in the room nor listen at the door. When they all came out – rather late at night – I took my chance. I thought I'd follow on behind them, far enough back so that I wouldn't be seen, and find out where they were going. I remember it as though it was yesterday. Mother had taken my clothes – she said for washing, but I have since thought it was more likely that she wanted to be sure I stayed at home under control; that meant that she then forgot about me and my absence wasn't noticed. When I heard them all go out, I grabbed the nearest thing to hand – a long linen sheet. The night air was warm and dry, so I thought it would do. Rather like a Roman toga, I told myself, as I wrapped it around me.

Jesus and eleven of the disciples went towards the city gate, past the Pool of Siloam, and along the Kidron Valley to the Garden of Gethsemane, part way up the Mount of Olives. (Judas wasn't with them: I had heard the noise of someone leaving the big room part way through the evening and that must have been him. It was a bit later that I learned why he had gone!) I couldn't get very near to the group, but I followed as closely as I could. I didn't hear all they said, but the air was still and their voices carried fairly well and I heard enough to make me feel I was with them. Jesus seemed very sad and rather depressed. The disciples had left our home singing a hymn, but as they walked Jesus said they would all desert him. He quoted scripture to them – Zechariah – where the prophet said: 'Strike the shepherd and the sheep will be scattered'. Jesus said it as though the prophet had been talking about him! But then he cheered up a bit and I distinctly heard him say, 'But after I have risen I will go before you into Galilee'. I couldn't make any sense of it at the time, but later, it was obvious.

When they got to the garden, I had to stay hidden. That wasn't difficult, since there were lots of trees about. It was quite an olive grove! Set on the side of the hill, there were young trees and some very old and gnarled ones, looking as though they had been there since the dawn of time. It was quite easy to be out of sight, but still be able to see all that was going on – and now I could get closer without fear of being seen. Most of the disciples sat about together on the ground, but Jesus took Peter, James and John further on, up the hill – almost out of earshot – and then he told them to watch and pray: he went on even further and I moved along with him. He couldn't see me, but I could hear him quite clearly now. He was worried and troubled and was praying that he might be permitted to avoid the impending troubles, but if he had to, he would bear it all – if it were what his Father wanted. It was a long wait. The other disciples were tired and went to sleep quite quickly, but Jesus obviously expected the 'three' to stay awake, to watch and pray for him. He came back to them three times and each time they had dozed off. Each time he came back, he woke them up and they didn't know what to say to him – he was worried and had stayed awake praying and they couldn't even stay awake! I must admit, I dozed a bit, too! Just as he was remonstrating with them for the third time and telling them that they might as well sleep on, I thought I could hear voices. Not the disciples', because the sound was too far away. Then I saw lights. There were people coming across the Kidron valley, from the Susa Gate, and they were coming up the pathway towards us! As they came closer I could see there were the chief priests, teachers of the Law and elders of the synagogue and with them were Temple guards and many others from the city, and leading them up towards us was – Judas! He went up to Jesus and embraced him! As he did so, the guards grabbed Jesus and the disciples started up to defend him. One even drew a sword and cut off the ear of Malchus, the servant of the high priest. Jesus told him to put up his sword – and healed Malchus' ear, too! In all the kerfuffle, the disciples seemed to realise that they were outnumbered and ran – further up the hillside, out of reach of the guards and towards other roads, which would take them away from the garden. I must have got a bit too close; in the excitement I had not been paying enough attention, because suddenly one of the guards grabbed at me, too! Fortunately, he held my linen winding sheet, which unwound very easily, letting me free to run – but absolutely naked! Still, better to save my skin, even though it was exposed for all the world to see. I got home breathless and crept through the garden to my room – and nobody knew I had been out. I lay on my bed, thinking of what had happened, of what might have happened and relieved that I did not have to explain where I had been, to Mother and Father – not yet – hopefully, never. I wondered what had happened to Jesus, but I didn't know how I would find out, because I wasn't supposed to know anything had happened. I eventually calmed down, my pulse settled and I fell asleep. The following morning started as any other day, but when Father came into the house at midday, he was very quiet and depressed. I overheard him telling Mother that Jesus had been arrested and taken to be crucified already! There was great concern about what might happen to anybody who was known to be a friend of Jesus, or a disciple, or one of the followers. I was confined to the house and garden again, because of the risk. Later that evening, after the Sabbath meal, after dark, someone called to see Father. Whoever it was did not stay long. After he had gone, Father got us all together and told us that Jesus had been crucified, but his body had been taken for burial by Joseph of Arimathea – a member of the council! He was buried in a new tomb (indeed, the workmen hadn't even finished cutting the rock of the roof on the inside at the back) in Joseph's garden. Mary of Magdala, and James and Joses' mother had watched Joseph and Nicodemus take his body into the tomb and close the entrance with the big stone – that could not have been easy for them, for they were both fairly elderly and stones used to close tomb entrances are huge, even though they are cut round to roll like a wheel. Everybody knew Joseph and everybody knew of his beautiful house and garden (though I didn't know anybody who had actually been inside it); it is on the other side of the city, but that's not far away – nowhere is 'very far away' in Jerusalem. It's not a big place.

Our house was at the southwestern corner of the city, not far from the house of the high priest, and my room was on the side of the house near the street. On the first day of the week, the morning after the Sabbath, very early in the morning, just after first light, I was woken by the sound of running feet and breathless, panicky voices. I got up and went to the window, but I couldn't make out who they were. They were too far away, near the high priest's house and the light was not good enough to see them clearly, but they were men's voices and they were saying something about what had happened at Jesus' tomb. Although it was barely dawn, I had to find out what was going on. I dressed quickly (the washing had been done and I had a clean white tunic to wear) and ran to Joseph of Arimathea's garden.

When I got there, I found a way in and could see the tomb (trespass is not a word that means much to a young man and I was far too excited to think about it, anyway); the great stone that had been rolled across the entrance was no longer there. It looked as though it had just been tossed back like a pebble – lying flat on the ground and some distance from the tomb itself, leaving the dark entrance to the tomb for all to see. Something really had happened! With pulse racing, I crept to the entrance and looked in. Nothing! No body there. Just the grave clothes, collapsed flat as though the body had just disintegrated within them. The headcloth had done the same thing, but it was separate from the rest, because it was not part of the winding sheet. Eerie is an understatement. All was still and quiet. I sat on the edge of the slab where the body had been, to get my breath back and to calm down; but then I heard voices approaching. This time they were women's voices. Not excited and noisy, like the voices that had woken me, but subdued and even though I could not see the women, they sounded nervous and hesitant. The chatter got louder as I sat thinking. Were they coming to this grave, expecting a body to be here? Then I could see them; they were carrying jars of spices for the preparation of a body and there was no other grave in the garden. There was no reason for women to be about in a private garden at that hour of the morning anyway, and if they were not of the household, they had no right to be there – any more than I had! But the body was not there. Had it been taken away already? Certainly not by that panic-stricken lot who had woken me. Neither could one imagine Joseph and Nicodemus moving the body again, after all that effort. But what was it that Jesus had said after he had left our home? 'After I have risen...' He had obviously risen from the dead!

By now, the women had almost reached the tomb and they, too, seemed surprised that the stone had been moved. As they neared the tomb, one of them saw me through the entrance. You have never seen such panic! I tried to explain, but they dropped the spices they were carrying and fled. I shouted after them that Jesus had said he would rise and would go ahead of them to Galilee, where they would see him. They should go and tell the others and Peter..., but I don't think they even heard me. I don't know whether they thought I was a ghost, a devil or an angel – but they didn't give me much chance to explain. Much later, there seemed to be rumours and stories of an angel, or two, at the tomb, but I think it was probably me they were talking about. I'm no angel, but I hope I never appear to be a devil to anybody.

This, of course, brings me to the reason for writing a treatise for the new believers. It is now some thirty-five years or so since Jesus died and rose again. Peter has, tragically, been killed recently, in Rome – crucified, like Jesus, though they say he insisted on being crucified upside down, as he was not worthy to die as his master had. We were not allowed anywhere near. The disciples had expected Jesus to return to earth whilst they were still alive, but James (the elder Zebedee) is dead – beheaded by Herod some twenty years ago, Peter is gone and Paul is in prison, in Rome, and under sentence of death. The stories and teachings of Jesus have been handed on by word of mouth – person to person – in the old style, but stories have a habit of changing in the telling, so I think it would be good – indeed important – to get things recorded as accurately as possible. So many amazing things happened during his life-time, let alone around the time of his death (that awful crucifixion fills me with horror whenever I think of it) and as I know how the story of his resurrection has become elaborated in its telling and re-telling, I feel I must write soon, before my memory becomes clouded or confused, or my life is imperilled. The teaching continues, perfectly well in the usual fashion, but there is nothing written down – apart from the letters from Paul. They have circulated around all the young churches and some have even been copied. But nothing has been written about the travels, teaching and works of Jesus! There is considerable unrest in Rome and if anything does happen to Paul, I think I might take up the suggestion of Apollos (when he was in Ephesus) and go to Alexandria: if I haven't finished the treatise by then, I can spend more time on it in greater safety there and complete my writing. You will probably know of Priscilla and Aquila – he was a leather-worker from Pontus and she a Roman lady – they had to get out of Rome quickly, some fifteen years ago, when the Emperor Claudius issued an edict expelling all Jews. They went to Corinth, at first, but then set up home in Ephesus; they went back to Rome for a while after the death of Claudius – but they had got used to the Ephesian way of life and now they are back there. I fear that there is the distinct risk that something similar will happen again, in Rome, and it may be that I will never get there again, or if I do, I may have to get out in a bit of a hurry.

I didn't really know Jesus, apart from seeing him with the others when they came to our home – as at their last supper together, as I've said. Peter did. Peter was there, with him. I travelled with Peter as a sort of disciple or assistant for years, after Paul and Uncle Barnabas' disagreement. I've listened to Peter preaching and teaching. He spoke of what Jesus did, what he said, how he said it and why. He talked of parables and miracles and had a way of bringing Jesus alive to those he was teaching. Peter! 'The Rock' Jesus had named him. He wasn't, at first, and he often recalled the way Jesus forgave him for all the things he did wrong, when they met after the resurrection. When Peter taught, he did not seem to forget even the simplest of things Jesus did and all this helped to explain who Jesus was and why he had come to live on earth. He was the first to recognise that Jesus was the Christ – the Holy One of Israel. I must get this all in writing before I forget. The way

Peter spoke was important; his conviction, his emphasis, his inspiration – all-important, themselves – and I must try to get this into my writing. But I'm not very good at writing, really. The others call me kolobodactylos – 'stumpy fingers' – they think my writing is clumsy. Still, good or bad, I must get it written, and soon.

I have been involved with the faith – The Way, as it is known – more or less since Jesus' resurrection. On the fringe, at first: youthful enthusiasm waxes and wanes! But then I became more involved. Uncle Barnabas (he was my cousin, really, but so much older than I that he was always known as 'uncle') had called Paul to join him at Antioch, to help him with a flourishing Gentile mission. This would be about fourteen or fifteen years after Jesus died. Uncle Barnabas and Paul were terrific – they made a tremendous team. Indeed, the followers of The Way became known as 'Christians' as a result. I thought that was rather clever: the followers of Jesus, the 'Christ'. Anyway, after that, Uncle Barnabas and Paul came to Jerusalem, after trekking around Judea helping the brethren hardest hit by the famine that year. They stayed with us for a while – that is how I learned about their travels – and when they were about to return to Antioch, they asked if I would like to go with them – to help. I was delighted and very flattered.

When we got to Antioch, we joined Simeon, Lucius and Manaen at a prayer meeting. During the time of worship, the Holy Spirit made it clear that Uncle Barnabas and Paul should go on a missionary journey, through Cyprus to the other Antioch, in Pisidia, and take in other towns nearby. That meant an enormous amount of preparation – it took nearly a year – and they suggested that I might like to go there, too, as a member of their team. The future looked very exciting for me.

When all was ready, we set off for Cyprus. We left Syrian Antioch and went south to Seleucia, on the coast. There we found the ship (it was a Roman grain ship whose captain was prepared to take passengers) that was to take us the 70 milia, or so, across to Cyprus. It meant setting sail very early in the morning, but with a favourable wind we could then make the crossing to the island in one day. Then, even if we were not able to land, we could anchor up in a sheltered bay for the night and make Salamis (the port we were heading for), which was quite a long way further down the southern coast, the following day. Cyprus is a pretty island with white sandy bays and a rocky, barren hinterland. We travelled throughout the island, from Salamis to Paphos, preaching in the synagogues and teaching outside. I found it all absolutely fascinating, but very tiring, particularly as Paul often talked late into the night and still expected everybody to be up early, fresh and ready for the next day's commitments. On one occasion we were summoned to meet the proconsul, Sergius Paulus, after we had confronted his attendant Elymas Bar-Jesus. The proconsul was an intelligent fellow, who was very interested in the faith and soon converted. Elymas was furious! He tried to turn Sergius Paulus away from Paul's teaching, but I shall never forget what happened when Paul looked at him – straight in the face – eye to eye: 'You are a child of the Devil', said Paul. 'The hand of the Lord is against you and you are going to be blind'. Immediately, Elymas became blind, groped around and had to have someone to lead him. When the proconsul saw this, he was flabbergasted! He was a 'convert' before, but now he was convinced that the faith was true.

From Paphos we sailed to Perga, in Pamphylia. Now I don't know whether it was the power that Paul had found that he had which had gone to his head, but long before we had sighted land he was beginning to get under my skin! I was about twentyeight years old, at that time and very much the junior member of the team, but Uncle Barnabas was the eldest; he was in his middle to late forties and Paul was little more than forty years old. Uncle Barnabas had called Paul to join the company and Paul was a recent convert compared with my uncle, but he seemed to be taking over the organisation! He was making the decisions. He was doing the planning. He was taking the credit. Uncle Barnabas was always very supportive and helpful, but it wasn't fair. We had not been in Perga very long before I felt that I had had enough. I talked to Uncle Barnabas, one night, and said I thought he should be in charge, but he said 'No'; he said he and I were the back-up team and Paul was the front man. He said that I was part of the team, and we all had to go the way the Spirit directed. That was all very well, but I couldn't stand Paul's arrogance. Uncle Barnabas said he would talk to Paul – and kept his word. There was a terrible row that evening. It was obvious that I was not helping towards the mission if I was responsible for so much friction, so I told Uncle Barnabas that I would return to Jerusalem. He was very understanding. He helped me to pack up my things and organised a working passage by boat, back home for me and came to see me off. It was a sad parting. I didn't know what the future held – for either of us.

It was a long, slow journey home. The boat called at every little port along the coast and by the time I got home I was absolutely exhausted – and then, what greeted me? The news had travelled ahead, somehow. When I got home, the rumour about was that I had left the missionary trip because I was homesick. You know how difficult it is to counter a well-established rumour. 'John Mark had come home to his mother' – well, I mean!

It was a couple of years later that Uncle Barnabas and Paul decided to go back to visit all the towns in which they had preached on their first tour. There was not so much excitement this time, as this was not going to be breaking new ground and making new converts, but it would be a lot of fun. Uncle Barnabas suggested to Paul that I should join them again. You would never believe the row that followed! The air was almost blue – and all my fault. Each called the other derogatory names and what Paul called me couldn't be put in writing. Christians! At least, that's what they are supposed to be. Eventually, they agreed to disagree. Paul would take Silas and visit the mainland towns and Uncle Barnabas could have me and go to his island of Cyprus! Anyway, I like Cyprus. It's pretty and friendly and there would not be so great a risk as travelling between towns in Syria and Cilicia – only the sea journey to worry about. It was a good tour and I learned a lot from Uncle Barnabas.

I suppose I changed over the intervening years, as a result of my experience. Paul, too, seemed to have appreciated the change – even at long range – and forgiven me, so that when Peter took me with him, to Rome, to preach as well, we saw much more of each other. Paul really must have thought I was now different, because about five years ago, when he was in prison and worried about the church in Colossae, he intended sending me on a missionary journey to the church there. Tychicus went, with a letter from Paul to tell them to expect me, but the trip didn't materialize. I don't know why, nor what happened. Nevertheless, Paul does seem to accept me now. I have just received information that he does not expect to be allowed to live much longer and he has sent a message, via Timothy in Ephesus, asking me to go to Rome to see him again. I must go, but, as I said, I am a bit concerned about the political situation. The Emperor obviously does not want Jews there. The trip will take some organising, too; there is not only the journey itself, but I shall have to get someone to take over here, in my absence. Timothy is based at Ephesus and between us we are responsible for the care of the young churches in Asia Minor, so it will not be easy to leave them. Still, I'm sure John will be able to help with the arrangements. All things are possible and the sooner I get on with it, the sooner we shall be able to make a start for Rome.

Somehow, I must also find time to get on with my writing, putting Peter's teaching into script. It is absolutely vital that Peter's experience is not lost, nor distorted in re-telling. Paul is the only one who has actually written anything, so far, and he didn't even know Jesus, when he was alive. Most of the disciples are dead – all having met tragic deaths – though we haven't had word of Matthew or Thomas for a long time. Matthew went to Ethiopia and Thomas travelled through Parthia and Persia and further beyond that. I didn't even know there were countries further to the east of Persia! But the last we heard was that he was still well and spreading the

Word to hitherto unknown peoples. Neither Matthew nor Thomas has put anything in writing, so far as I know. John is well; he has been living in and around Ephesus and teaching throughout Asia Minor, but we have been keeping in close touch and I know he hasn't written anything. Someone must write so that all the churches can read about Jesus. We must have written facts, so that nothing can be distorted in the telling, available to teach all the world, now and for generations to come. I think I shall call my treatise the 'Good News' – according to Mark, of course!

Luke

The Doctor

Luke

The Doctor

I am a physician: I trained at our medical school in Philippi as a result of the generosity of my mentor Theophilus. It is a good school in the Greek tradition, though small and not so well known as those in Athens and Alexandria.

Medical training – from the earliest stage – indoctrinates one with the need to seek out all the available facts before coming to a diagnosis. One has, therefore, to abide by several established principles.

The first is to take an adequate history – the story relating to the patient's problem – perhaps from some time in the distant past, right up to the present. It is important to let the patient talk and to record what is said in the way it is said. This might not result in the most erudite grammar, nor sophisticated expression, but the patient's mode of expression may convey as much information as the words used. In addition, one may prod the patient's memory by direct questioning, but this technique is only used later – to check possible lines for further investigation. The language of medicine, where I trained, is Greek. Although my colleagues and I were required to write and speak correctly, we were never criticised for recording in the local phraseology. For some this was easy, since they were slaves put to study medicine by a generous and affluent master. Others were 'freedmen' and many were of more noble origin; for them the local vernacular was both literally and grammatically foreign.

The second principle is to examine thoroughly. All parts must be checked, lest something of importance may be missed. If one examines with preconceived ideas, many important signs – either present or absent – will not be available to critical thought and misinterpretations may lead to false conclusions being drawn.

Thirdly, special investigations or examinations may be indicated, perhaps to examine the depth of redness in a bloodstained piece of linen, to assess the colour and odour of vomit, to taste for the presence of sugar in the urine or to look for parasites in the faeces.

Lastly, a 'test of cure' may be helpful – herbs or tinctures may be used and the response in the patient's state of health observed.

These principles may seem to be appropriate only to medicine, but I assure you that they are equally applicable if one is to investigate, and record for posterity, a locality, a historical event of major importance, a political movement or a groundswell of popular opinion. What eyewitnesses say, the way they individually describe a happening, will all be slightly different, but all will add colour and authenticity to any record – be it specifically medical, scientific or historical. Needless to say, I have employed all these basic principles in my investigations and recording of the early times of the Lord's life, his ministry, his teaching, his followers and the incredible changes in the lives of those who knew him or who learned about him.

I shall eternally regret never having met the Lord, but I count it the greatest of privileges that I have been associated, from the earliest days, with Christianity (the title produced for the belief of the followers of The Way in Antioch, my family's home town, in Syria), of having known Paul, the other leaders of the faith and of having had the honour of talking to Mary, the mother of the Lord. My father had been the slave of a Roman tribune and, generously, had been given his freedom as a wedding present when he married my mother, the handmaid of the tribune's wife. I still have relatives in Antioch and I travel to visit them fairly frequently. It was whilst I was making one of these family duty visits that I first heard of the strange and exciting happenings in Palestine. I was absolutely fascinated and after closer investigation I became convinced of their reliability, converted and have been a follower of The Way myself ever since. This must have been two or three years before I first met Saul Paullus himself.

After I had completed my training, I established a practice (with colleagues) in Philippi, where I have set up my home. I recall the occasion when my colleagues and I first heard of miraculous healings in Troas. We were told of patients with serious, potentially fatal illnesses who were cured. They were not simply improved, but were made completely well – and, by all accounts, they were not being healed by trained and qualified physicians. After a lengthy discussion, I was delegated by my colleagues to travel to Troas to investigate what was going on and they agreed to look after my practice for a short time. I was quite happy with the arrangement. I enjoy travelling; the busy little ports, typical smells (some pleasant and others not so!), ships and the sea itself, the vastness of it, its unpredictability and its overwhelming, awesome power – but I digress.

When I arrived in Troas I chanced to hear that Saul Paullus was expected in the city on another of his journeys to spread the new teaching. I also learned that he needed to consult a physician, so I made it my business to let it be known that I was again in the city and available for consultation. He had been troubled by a recurrent eye inflammation[1] from the time of his conversion on the Damascus road; it appeared to be the eye disease very commonly found in the countries bordering the Great Sea, to the South and East. It causes pain, discharge, 'crusting', scarring and causes the eyelids and eyelashes to invert, resulting in irritation, ulceration, facial disfigurement, deterioration of sight and, ultimately, blindness. I applied the 'blue rock stick' to the inner aspects of his eyelids and prescribed a medicated eye-wash for him to use – not a very complicated treatment, but it does slow the progress of the disease. He was already experiencing problems with his vision and had had to use the services of an amanuensis to write his letter to the Galatian churches; he only wrote the conclusion to the letter in his own hand – and that with some difficulty! After the formal consultation, we talked of The Way and the Lord. We discussed the need to spread the Word to the Gentile world and I explained to him our need in Macedonia. At Philippi we didn't have many Jews, let alone Christians, and most of the Jews were women. There wasn't even a synagogue for them, though the religious formalities only

---

[1] This was probably the disease we now know as Trachoma

required the regular worship of ten devout Jewish men for one to be established. They weren't even allowed to have a formal meeting house. The women usually met for prayers near the bank of the river Gangites. Paul and I talked well into the evening and he explained to me that the miraculous healings that I had come to investigate were through faith and were happening with believers through the power of the Lord and in his name. It was very late before we were aware of it, so I invited Paul and his companion Silas to stay with me at the inn. I was delighted, the following morning, when Paul told me that the Lord had given him a vision during the night, instructing him to come to Macedonia and he agreed to come back with me that very day.

We sailed from Troas as soon as we could find a ship to take us. It is more than a day's sailing – even with the best wind – to Neapolis (which is the seaport access to Philippi), so we anchored off Samothrace for the night. This is a very rocky and mountainous little island, but there are several very pleasant and sheltered bays, in its lee, that offer safe anchorage. The following day we made Neapolis without a problem late in the afternoon. It is a little less than 10 milia to Philippi along the Via Egnatia – not too far to walk, if one has an early start, but not at that time of day – so we hired horses and arrived home in time for a very welcome evening meal and rest. It was good to have Paul and Silas break bread with me at my home.

The following day, being the Sabbath, I took Paul and Silas to the women's meeting place for prayer and introduced them to the group. Lydia, one of the well-known businesswomen, who was herself a Jewish convert, was most impressed by Paul's speaking and teaching. She declared herself a

convert to The Way and insisted that we should all go
to her home and stay with her, rather than put up at
a local inn. This was not only exciting, but was most
opportune, since it gave me the chance to leave Paul
in good company whilst I discussed my findings in
Troas with my colleagues. They were somewhat
sceptical about faith healing, but were prepared to
accept my word that no other explanation seemed
plausible. They also agreed to look after my practice
for a while longer, whilst I felt committed to
entertaining and keeping company with my most
distinguished visitors. I had the feeling, however,
that they thought I was rather overawed by this
physically unimpressive apostle of a crucified
carpenter – and a tent-maker by trade – to boot.
Their concerns were somewhat more forcefully
expressed when, after Paul expelled a demon from a
young prophetess and converted her to The Way,
thereby ruining the business of her owner, he and
Silas were imprisoned. There was little I could do to
help, but I gathered that the authorities were very
worried for a while when they realised that they had
beaten and imprisoned a Roman citizen! Paul seemed
to think it had all been worthwhile, however, since
the jailer and his family were converted as a result.
When they were released, Lydia insisted that Paul
and Silas should stay with her for a while, to regain
their composure. They left, in due course, to go on
towards Amphipolis and Apollonia, heading for
Thessalonica some 100 milia away. I, sadly, returned
to my somewhat neglected practice.

Paul seemed to have had a propensity for being
involved in riots: there was another in Thessalonica!
This time he and Silas were accused of treason and
Jason and the other brothers were bound over to give

guarantees that Paul and Silas would leave town without causing further trouble and never return. Similarly, in Berea, the brothers had to send Paul away to the coast to avoid an outbreak of violence! In Corinth there was nearly another, but the Jews had to take Paul to court, where the proconsul, Gallio, threw out their case, telling them he was not prepared to listen as no crime had been committed.

I kept in touch with Paul whilst he trekked on through Macedonia and Achaia: he went by sea to Athens, on to Corinth, but then he sent word that he was going back to Jerusalem. In fact, when he eventually got there, he travelled on north again to Syrian Antioch, where he stayed for about six months or so. Then he was off on his travels again, intending to revisit the places to which he had been when on his first two major journeys – back to Galatia, Phrygia, and Ephesus in particular where, indeed, he stayed for quite a long time. Whilst there, Paul determined to return to Macedonia and Achaia, before going back to Jerusalem again, and then to go on to Rome itself. He wrote to me from Ephesus to tell me of his plans and invited me to join him: this time I not only knew I would meet him, but I had the chance to make plans. This time, I told my colleagues, I was going to be away for some while. They were not happy with this arrangement, but agreed that the income from my patients would pay for a junior, in my absence, and they would be available for advice, when necessary. Neither they nor I realised, at that stage, quite how long I was going to be away.

When I had all my professional arrangements sorted out, I decided that I would travel to Ephesus to join Paul, rather than await his arrival in Macedonia and I was fortunate in finding a boat going across to Troas and then on to Ephesus with her cargo. The master had only a few passengers, so I was able to book a passage all the way. It is a much longer sea voyage than I had ever undertaken before, both in distance and time, but I had not realised how different the travelling would be, by comparison with the relatively straightforward crossing from Neapolis to Troas. The journey was slow. The sailing wind generally blows from early morning until late afternoon, so there is the repeated need to anchor up each night. But these are all coastal craft – rarely, if ever, out of sight of land and as the ship passes between the islands, the wind changes direction so frequently – even to the extent of almost being taken aback, at times – that there is the constant need to re-set sails. This is not only hard on the sailors, but it slows the journey down even more. Still, there was no great pressure on time and, as I have said, I enjoy the sea. Ephesus is still a major city, although her importance as a commercial centre is waning – much as her importance as a port is declining. The river Meander brings down masses of silt and debris from the mountains; indeed, if they do not clear the approach to the harbour soon, it will silt up completely and shipping will not be able to get into the port at all.

Ephesus has always been associated with some cult or other. Artemis (or Diana as the Romans call her) is the present goddess and she is the source of much of the local trade and commerce. Indeed, it was this association that got Paul involved in yet another riot (three months or so after I had joined him there) and prompted his departure from the district after he had been in the city for more than two and a half years!

As I said, much of the local commerce related to Artemis: visitors and sightseers bought trinkets and artefacts made by the silversmiths and also contributed donations when visiting the shrines. Even the local butchers had a flourishing trade in 'sacrificial meat'. Little wonder then that when Paul was expounding the new teaching, the local tradesmen and artisans found an impact on their incomes. This all culminated in a riot led by one Demetrius – a silversmith and skilled rabble-rouser – who attacked Paul, saying that he was teaching that 'man-made gods are no gods at all'. Since all were dependent on the great goddess Artemis in some way, it was easy for him to raise them to fury very quickly. People poured out into the Arcadian Way from the harbour, from their stalls and from their homes, all storming along the colonnaded route towards the vast theatre. The theatre itself could hold about 25,000 people and it seemed that 25,000 people were there, shouting and screaming for Paul's blood! They had found Paul's travelling companions, Gaius (a convert from Derbe) and Aristarchus (from Thessalonica), and had dragged them into the theatre and were obviously trying to hold them as being at least partly responsible for the trouble. Alexander was pushed to the front in an attempt to defend Gaius and Aristarchus and placate the crowd, but when they realised he was a Jew, the uproar got even worse. If it had not been for the City Clerk, I fear they might all have been torn limb from limb. He really was superb! He had such a powerful personality that his very presence quietened the crowd. He told them, in a very quiet and measured voice, that it was undeniable that Ephesus was the guardian of Artemis' temple, but neither Gaius nor

Aristarchus had blasphemed the name of Artemis, nor had they robbed her temple and they were, therefore, guilty of nothing. If Demetrius had a private grievance, then he had recourse to the courts, but nothing could justify the public chaos he had caused. Furthermore, unless the citizens of Ephesus dispersed quickly, they would be at risk of charges of civil disobedience! I have never seen a crowd quietened so quickly. The theatre emptied almost as quickly as it had filled, the people murmuring amongst themselves that Demetrius had best be more circumspect with his accusations in future and not put the entire populace at risk of legal action. Calm was restored, but it was this rather unfortunate episode which expedited Paul's departure, leaving the brothers from Ephesus worried about their future in a city which was becoming increasingly hostile.

Paul sent out for all of them to come and see him before he left. All came within a day or so and there was great sorrow and concern, both for their future and for him in his travels. Paul exhorted them to hold on to the Faith, despite all the difficulties with which they would have to contend. So, with great hugs and well-wishing and their hopes to see Paul again soon, we left to go on to Troas. Little did we know, at that time, that we would never return to Ephesus. I have rarely seen Paul in such a state of agitation as at that time. His eyesight had deteriorated further and he had developed a recurrent fever, but it did not seem that worry about his medical problems was the cause. Could it have been that the riot had had a much greater impact than I had expected, or was it his concern for the brothers we were leaving and his anxiety to meet Titus in Troas with a report from his beloved, worrisome

Corinth and what it might contain? Matters were made worse when we arrived at Troas – Titus wasn't there! I tried to persuade Paul to wait, as I was quite sure my cousin would have sent word, if he was unduly delayed or not able to get to Troas for some reason. Paul would have none of it. So great was his state of agitation that we had to go on to Philippi to find Titus – and there was nothing I could do to stop him.

To sea again! It seemed that I was becoming a very frequent traveller, between Troas and Philippi – some of the regular sea-farers at Neapolis were even beginning to recognise me. By the time we got to Philippi, word was there that Titus was on his way and, indeed, he arrived a few days later. At last Paul relaxed. Sight of Titus and the comforting news he brought from Corinth was a better relaxant than any of the medicaments I had offered him over the past week or more – even if I had succeeded in getting any past his lips.

It was good to see my cousin again – we are good friends as well as being related and the two do not necessarily follow as the night follows the day. We had a lot of catching-up to do, as we hadn't seen each other for quite some time. Paul, however, got down to writing his fourth treatise[2] to the church in Corinth. When part way through this, word came that the 'Judaising missionaries' had reached Corinth, after leaving Galatia, and were leading another attack on his teaching. He finished the letter as quickly as he could and Titus was charged with taking it ahead of Paul, back to Corinth with all haste. Paul felt that he should continue teaching in Philippi

---

[2] This was the letter which we know as his second letter to the Corinthians.

for a while and then travel around Macedonia, before spending the winter months in Greece. We had a number of brothers with us, including Gaius, young Timothy from Lystra, Trophimus from Ephesus and Tychicus the Asian, so Paul suggested that I should travel with Titus: two, travelling in company, always provide support for each other. We set off together, somewhat apprehensively in the light of the news about the Judaisers – but we needn't have worried.

It was late summer – almost autumn – and although the journey was long, it was very pleasant and uneventful. We didn't travel in the heat of the day, but since, at that time of the year, the heat of the day is relatively short, we managed to travel comfortably and covered reasonable distance during daylight hours. When we reached Corinth, we were relieved and pleasantly surprised to find that, despite all the foreboding, many of the brothers had held firm and Paul's letter was a great encouragement to them. They were delighted to learn that Paul was to follow us and that he intended spending the winter in Corinth. After a while Paul arrived bringing with him Sopater from Macedonia, Aristarchus and Secundus the Thessalonians, in addition to the others. Paul immediately set to, with preaching and teaching to counter the Judaisers' mischief. It was a great success: those who had wavered were re-stabilised and those who had not, were strengthened in the Faith. Paul stayed at the home of Gaius over the winter months and the brothers who had travelled with him, stayed with other members of the church in Corinth. I find it difficult to work and write unless I am on my own, so I took lodgings at a local inn, where I could both write and keep in touch with the others in the party. Paul wrote too: he felt reassured and satisfied with the success of the mission and concentrated on composing his great missive to the Roman church. He had an excellent amanuensis in Tertius who was not only a friend, but both a Christian and a professional secretary as well.

With the approach of spring, Paul began to talk of finally leaving Greece and returning to Jerusalem. He could be a most obstinate character! Leaving Greece was all very well: the young churches now seemed fairly secure in their beliefs, but we could not convince Paul that the Jews in these cities now bore him a grudge and would take any opportunity to avenge their hurt – the episode in Gallio's court remained to the forefront of their minds! We could not believe his naïve simplicity, when he announced plans to travel on his own, by sea, to Ephesus in the pilgrim ship. Sheer suicide! It would be absolutely filled with scheming, plotting, resentful Jews: it was only when we showed him evidence of a plan to kill him and despatch his body overboard that he actually listened. He agreed to retrace his steps to Philippi and sail for Troas from Neapolis – we could all accompany him overland and the familiar sea route would be both shorter and safer. In the event, however, it was a slow crossing; the headwinds were formidable and it took us five days to cross.

Troas, yet again! But this time I really did witness the impossible. I can vouch for it with my life. Paul, in his usual fashion on the first day of the week, met with the brethren at Troas to break bread with them and to teach. The meeting had begun in the latter part of the day; the weather was not yet hot, but winter had passed and it was comfortably warm. In that upper room, however, there were many people crammed into the small space, oil-lamps were burning and the atmosphere became hot and heavy. Although we listened to Paul fascinated, not missing a word, young Eutychus must have thought he was droning on interminably! I caught his eye once or twice, but then noticed his eyelids drooping. Suddenly, Paul was stopped in mid-sentence by a scream from one of the women. Eutychus had been sitting in the window space – and he just disappeared! The men nearest the stairway ran down and found him in the courtyard below – dead! I know. I saw it all. I was there. I have had to certify death often enough to go through the usual 'check routine' automatically. He was dead: no movement, no breathing, no pulse, no heartbeat. Then Paul came down, distraught that he had been the cause of young Eutychus' fall. But then, all he said was 'Don't worry. He's alright'. He couldn't be – he was dead – but then he got up and we all returned: Eutychus to his window seat and Paul to finish his sermon! My colleagues had sent me from Philippi to investigate the rumours of strange healings – if only they could have seen what I had seen!

We had not been in Troas long, before Paul began to get anxious. He wanted to move on: his aim was to return to Jerusalem and be there in time for Pentecost – but travel for such a journey required considerable organisation. We managed to find passage on a ship that was sailing to Patara, on the coast of Lycia, so we were to be away from Troas within the week. In the day or so before we left, Paul became very thoughtful and introspective. Then, out of the blue, he announced that he would walk, alone, across the headland and meet with us at Assos! Why? That wild, exposed headland road is dangerous. It is uninhabited, rocky country and there is always the risk of being attacked by bandits. Almost as bad, I discovered later, as the road from Jerusalem to Jericho – renowned for bandit attacks. We tried to persuade him not to go, or at least, not to go alone, but he would have none of it. Indeed, he can be obstinate! I think, perhaps, he felt he was going to Jerusalem for the last time, as his Master had, before him. Perhaps this was to be his time with God, as the Lord had spent time in Gethsemane before his trial. I shall never know; I asked him why, before he set out, and several times after, but each time he changed the subject. I can hardly express the relief we all experienced when he did eventually join us at Assos late that evening. There is some good Roman road towards the headland, but it is more than 35 milia and much of his journey would, therefore, have to be in the heat of the day. It is at least twice as far by sea, around Cape Lectum, but we had a good wind and reached port by early afternoon; he did not even set out until after we had left and we had boarded the ship at sunrise. In typical fashion, he came to the ship to make sure all was well and didn't leave the quay until we had slipped the moorings. We later discovered that he also went to see Eutychus, before setting out, to ensure he was well!

I had thought that we might sail on, once we had Paul on board, although it was late in the day. Mitylene is on the eastern side of Lesbos and is a straight run with the wind from Assos, but the captain refused to set sail for fear of losing the wind before reaching there. The prevailing wind is a favourable northerly but, as I have said, sailing is limited because it only blows from about dawn to late afternoon: by sunset the stillness is palpable. We, therefore, made the most of the quayside town and had a good meal – at least Paul had chance to rest and recover.

The following day we sailed to Mitylene, where the captain had business to undertake, so we did not sail on from there until the next day. This was somewhat frustrating, but the journey was going to be a whole sequence of stopping and sailing, so I resigned myself to enjoying the trip. I do enjoy travelling, particularly by sea, so I had the pleasure of an interesting journey, glorious coastal views and fascinating new ports and harbours to visit – quite apart from the company of good friends on board. With a favourable wind and open water, we could expect to sail at least 60 milia each day and we did have good weather and a favourable wind from Mitylene to Khios. Some of our day was in open sea – never out of sight of land – but for the last 30 milia or so, towards the anchorage off Khios, there were many pretty little islands so travel was much slower, as I've explained. When we were within the sound, with the mainland peninsular to the east and Khios itself to the west, I became concerned that around these little islands there were rocky shoals below the water-line, which could tear the bottom from our boat! Our captain, however, knew the passage well – he had travelled it often enough to know the deep-water channels and the danger areas. We were in good hands. We anchored off, in the sound: since we had no need to land, the captain did not wish to incur harbour dues. At sunrise the following day, we weighed anchor and sailed for Samos, the main port of the island of the same name and the next day we had a short run to Miletus, the mainland harbour in the mouth of the river Meander.

We had completely bypassed Ephesus. Now I am aware that the harbour at Ephesus is not well maintained and is silting up, but our ship was not large and even when loaded did not have great a draught and it should have been possible to have reached the town quay. Whether the captain felt the risk was too great, or whether – because of the trouble he had had when last there – Paul wished to avoid the city himself, I could not determine, but I do know that it took the greater part of three days for the elders at Ephesus to come to Miletus to see Paul. He was anxious to see them and sent a message to say that this was the last chance he would have to greet them in person. It was a very emotional time. Paul talked to them at great length: the Jews at Ephesus had started a smear campaign against him after he last left Ephesus and Paul wanted to re-emphasise that he hadn't changed. He explained to them that he had to go to Jerusalem – the Holy Spirit was directing him there – but he did not know what to expect, although trouble was most likely. He exhorted them to stand firm in the Faith and be watchful for dissenters – even from within their own company.

After talking to them for some while, he committed them to God, encouraged them to keep up their practical trades so that they would always be able to earn enough – not only for their own survival, but so that they would also be able to support brethren incapable of earning. Finally, we prayed together and then tried to leave We literally had to tear ourselves away from them – they clung to Paul, weeping and tearing their clothes in great distress. They held on to us, as though keeping us prisoners would deflect Paul from his intent to go to Jerusalem.

Were we not going directly to our ship, I'm sure they would have tried to lay siege to us at the inn! We put to sea, sailing for the island of Cos, and they stood on the quayside, at least until we could no longer see the harbour! We did not reach the island until late in the afternoon, since we had not sailed at sunrise, so we spent the night at the town of Cos itself. It surprises me that although these coastal towns have a marked similarity – harbours, quays, store-houses, inns and private dwellings – they are all different, with their own recognisable characteristics, styles, smells and even dialects. Even the little local boats are easily identifiable with their ports of origin.

At sunrise the next day, we sailed for Rhodes (again passing many fascinating little islands), which was to be our last island mooring for a long time to come. We reached harbour just before the wind dropped, and Paul and I talked at great length about what we should have to do the following day. There should be no problem reaching Patara, even if the wind proved to be unfavourable, but we would then have to find a ship crossing to Palestine and that would probably mean getting further to the east along the coast, to Myra. Much of the major shipping crossing from Asia to Egypt, Syria or Palestine sailed from Myra, so we should probably waste least time by planning a journey by the coastal road, after disembarking at Patara – a journey of some 50 to 60 milia – unless, of course, we were fortunate enough to find a small boat ready to sail along the coast, just as we landed. Titus and I were commissioned to find transport to Palestine – and indeed we did. When we had berthed, we found that there was a huge galley, already almost completely loaded, due to sail the next day to Phoenicia – from Patara itself. The master had already taken on some passengers, but agreed to take our party as well – seven others, apart from Paul and myself (Aristarchus, Secundus, Sopater, Timothy, Titus, Tychicus and Trophimus). This was certainly good fortune, since she was to discharge most of her cargo at Tyre and then sail on to Ptolemais a little further to the south. We all boarded that evening: our accommodation was quite good, though rather expensive, I thought. I believe the master felt it was safe for him to increase the fare, since we had a fairly large party and all needed to travel together – and soon – and from Patara.

When I awoke the following morning we were already under sail, with the land fast disappearing off the larboard beam. This was to be the longest sea voyage I had made, so far. The journey to Tyre is about 400 milia, but this time there was to be no mooring at night. The winds were still mostly favourable during the day, but now we travelled continuously, under sail and oar when the wind blew, and care of the galley slaves alone, when it didn't. Many galley masters are hard and unfeeling men who literally drive their slaves to death. Ours seemed to be somewhat more considerate – I was asked to see and treat one of the slaves who had developed diarrhoea: this can be very dangerous, especially to an individual at sea, since fresh water is in limited supply and dehydration can kill. Also, if it is due to some contagion, it can spread throughout the entire ship, endangering slaves, crew and passengers alike.

We were out of sight of land completely for much of the journey: we did sight Cyprus, away off to larboard, as we sailed below her south-western shore. Land! Even the fleeting glimpse of an island, when travelling by sea, is very reassuring! It is easy to feel that one is sailing off the edge of the world, as hour after hour goes by, surrounded by nothing but water. Although one is aware that the master of the ship can navigate by the sun and stars, and that he has made the same journey many times before, the feeling of isolation, when surrounded by water, can only be understood by those who have actually experienced it.

At last, after little more than three days from Myra, we sighted land. The city of Tyre itself stands on an island peninsula with two harbours: the island one facing the mainland and that on the mainland protected by the causeway, both thus being sheltered from storms from any direction. As we stood at the ship's rail, Tyre grew larger and larger and more and more reassuring. Terra firma at last! I have now sailed in many ships of varying sizes – some fairly big and many smaller – and having watched them berthed, it does not appear to be too difficult a task. One almost feels capable of undertaking the procedure oneself. But berthing a galley, the size of ours, requires real skill – plus the co-operation, knowledge and confidence of the crew. A vessel of that size does not stop easily. The master was superb! We came alongside the quay and moored with hardly a bump. It was going to be a long time whilst her cargo was unloaded, even working by day and night, and she would still have to take on further cargo for Ptolemais.

In the event, we were in Tyre for a week, so there was ample time to meet the disciples living there. Indeed, we could have gone on by road more quickly than the delay for enshipment, but the brothers were so overjoyed to see Paul again that it was all worthwhile. They urged him, repeatedly, not to go to Jerusalem, however. They were sure he would meet trouble, at least – if not worse. Paul was, nevertheless, convinced that the Spirit wished him to go on, whatever the risk. Parting from that crowd was reminiscent of the parting from the Ephesian elders at Miletus. Wives, children and all came to see us off, as we boarded to set sail for Ptolemais. There was much chatter as we walked to the quayside. Tears, fears, worries, concern, love, good wishes – and still the exhortation not to go! We prayed together and after a final, final farewell, we were at sea again – for the day's journey to Ptolemais.

Another port, another meeting with the local disciples. Paul seemed enthusiastic, encouraged and refreshed with each meeting, but I have to admit that I find it incredibly difficult to cope with. I am a doctor – my profession requires that one remains emotionally detached from the patient, so that the very best of care can be provided dispassionately. A doctor must not become emotionally involved with his patient and I found it distinctly draining to be so involved, so often.

We spent no more than a day in Ptolemais. I was given the task of deciding the best means of travel to Jerusalem and I found a ship preparing to sail the next day to Caesarea – from there we would have to travel by road – there was no port nearer to our destination than Caesarea. I did not look forward to that journey: it is more than 60 milia and much of the road is through hill country, where there is a high risk of being attacked by robbers. Still, we were a fairly large party and there is always safety in numbers. When the time came, a large company of the disciples from Caesarea insisted on coming with us to ensure our safety. There were the now familiar farewells at Tyre, a short day's sailing, and we arrived at Caesarea.

Caesarea. What a port! It was built by Herod the Great some eighty years earlier (about twenty years, or so, before our Lord was born), with no expense spared. Jerusalem is inland and there was no easily accessible port for either political or commercial purposes. Herod decided that a port was vital, settled on a small non-descript fishing village as being an acceptable location and turned it into this magnificent city. It was here that we met Philip. Philip was known as the Evangelist – one of the Chosen Seven – a delightful character. He was friendly, enthusiastic, full of drive and determination. He had settled in the city, some twenty years or so earlier, with his young family: his four daughters were now grown up and were handsome women, all dedicated to The Way, none married and all having prophetic gifts of the Spirit. This, for me, was the experience of a lifetime. Philip and Stephen were involved with the disciples and The Way, much earlier even than Paul. I learned so much during the time that Paul and I stayed with them – from Philip himself, and stories that his daughters (particularly his prettily charming youngest daughter – who also seemed to want to talk about my profession of medicine) related about their father and the experiences that he had discussed with them. We stayed with them, as their guests, for about four days at this stage, but I returned to stay with them again later, when Paul was imprisoned.

The first evening we were there was fairly formal, but by the second, Philip relaxed with us and really chattered! He enjoyed talking. He was, after all, the Evangelist. He talked about the decision (and need) to select the Seven; he talked about the Twelve – and Matthias, and his election. He related stories about the Lord, if not at first hand, at least directly told to him by one or other of the Twelve. Most particularly, he told me of Stephen: his dedication, his selection, his youthful enthusiasm – and his death. By now, I had been with Paul a long time and travelled many milia with him, but not once did he elaborate on that happening, apart from acknowledging that he was there, giving witness and approval to the stoning. Philip told of Stephen's oration and assault on the establishment, and the fury this generated in the Jews. Stephen died knowing that he was going to be with his Lord.

The third evening, after dinner, the girls got their father talking again. He told us of his mission to Samaria and of success in casting out evil spirits and healing the sick in the name of Jesus and of the encounter with Simon the Sorcerer. Simon sounded as though he had been rather self-confident, conceited, thought that he had divine power and felt that he was someone great. Such was the success of the preaching, however, that even Simon was converted. He was baptised and, like a slave, followed Philip around everywhere. From the earliest times, the 'bush telegraph' has always been the fastest means of news travelling and the success of the preaching in Samaria and the conversions to The Way rapidly brought Simon Peter and John from Jerusalem to see what was really going on. There were many, many converts. Peter and John prayed for them, laid hands on them and gave them the new 'gift of the Holy Spirit'.

It was, though, Philip's experience with the Ethiopian eunuch that fascinated me. I have been a believer, now, for a long time, but I have never, personally, known direct instruction from the Holy Spirit, the Lord nor his angels – except when Paul had been told, in Troas, to go with me to Macedonia, but that was nothing special, so far as I was concerned. Philip's second daughter told us how she was awakened from sleep one night, when they were living in Sebaste in northern Samaria, at the end of the mission. She was about twelve years old, at the time. She had woken just before first light, had heard her father moving about and had gone to find out what was the matter. She thought that he might be unwell. He told her that an angel of the Lord had told him to get up and hurry south. Without questioning, she got some food and drink prepared whilst he went to waken the owner of the local livery stables: he wanted the fastest, most reliable horse he could hire. Philip is a good horseman (even his name suggests it) and having collected the provisions from his daughter, he left, simply saying that he had to ride south, towards the cross-roads on the road from Jerusalem to Gaza – some 60 to 70 milia away. He didn't know why he had to go, how long he would be away, nor what he would find when he got there – but he had to travel fast!

As I have said before, the road to Jerusalem is dangerous for a lone traveller, but most people would say the speed of Philip's horses probably kept him out of trouble; Philip knew that if the Spirit was sending him, he would be protected. He changed horses at another livery he had used before, about half-way to Jerusalem in the western foothills of Samaria. Then a further change of mount on the Damascus road – within sight of the city – then to the west, past Golgotha, and then south towards Bethlehem on the old Gaza road. Ahead, he could see a dust cloud – travellers going south. He caught up and joined the company, as was the acceptable practice for a lone traveller, and discovered that this was the party of an Ethiopian eunuch. He was the Chancellor of the Treasury of Queen Candace, returning to her court and home, and was reading from a scroll of the Prophet Isaiah. He did not understand the passage he was reading and asked if Philip could explain it – at last, the reason for the Lord sending him on that long journey! They talked together for some time, Philip teaching and answering questions, and then the Ethiopian asked Philip for baptism! Since there was a river nearby, the entire company witnessed the ceremony. They were near the crossroads, at Bethsura, but such was the excitement and celebration over the baptism that the Ethiopian party probably didn't even notice Philip leave them. He took the road west towards Azotus (again on the instruction of the Spirit) and made his way back to Caesarea Maritime, preaching and teaching on the way. He felt then that he needed to make Caesarea his base: his wife and daughters made the necessary arrangements and all the family moved to join him.

We talked late into the night. I enjoyed the company of the girls – not really surprising, since I had been almost exclusively in male company for well over a year and a half. Yes, there were the serving maids at the inns where we stayed, but apart from pleasant chatter, they offered little more. The only other females were the prostitutes, plying their trade (at inns or elsewhere) and they were best avoided. I have had too many patients who had succumbed to their charms and ended up with problems passing urine – pain, urgency, frequency – and even blindness, for some of them; and all for a short time of pleasure. Not only that, but their wives often seemed to be barren and that (particularly for the Jews) was a social disaster as well as the practical one of having no one to help with the family business.

Philip's daughters were bright, intelligent, humorous and stimulating of thought and discussion. The evening was near gone when I realised that we were intending travelling to Jerusalem the following day. Jerusalem! The risky journey and the worry as to what we could expect when we arrived. We all felt that Paul was running too great a risk and the feeling was re-enforced by the prophet Agabus; he had come down from Judea and like a latter-day Jeremiah, suggested that to go to Jerusalem would be to make a doomsday journey. He did a little mime, taking Paul's waist sash and binding his hands and feet with it, saying that the Holy Spirit had told him that this is what would happen to the owner of the sash in Jerusalem. The Jews would bind him and hand him over to the Gentiles. Still, Paul would have none of it. To Jerusalem we were going, whatever the risk; nothing and no-one would make him change his mind, even if he was to die as a result! There was no point in further persuasion, so we gave up. At least – as I have said – many of the brothers at Caesarea insisted on travelling with us, so we were a fairly large party and the risk of being attacked by robbers was significantly reduced. Nevertheless, it was about 65 milia from Caesarea Maritime to Jerusalem, a two-day trek, and I was beginning to hate horses! Each time I think of that journey I am impressed by the way Philip managed to cover the same ground, at that speed and meet up with the Ethiopian party at just the right spot on the road. We hired beasts from the livery stables Philip used most often – pack horses for the baggage and others for us to ride. I viewed the prospect with apprehension. I have never been very happy on horseback. I did not learn to ride until after I had qualified in medicine and then I usually managed to find more comfortable transport when visiting my patients. One feels so high off the ground and dependent on an animal with a will of its own. I have treated many men for injuries sustained when thrown from their horses. I do not altogether trust the animal to do what it is bidden: I suppose that may make the horse uncertain, too. Anyhow, we set off at about the third hour on a beautifully clear day, towards Jerusalem. The first day passed uneventfully and we stopped at a small village, where we found a comfortable inn. The fact that we had been travelling through dangerous countryside worried me less than the way we had been travelling. After all, we were a large group, with all the brothers. Oh, but that ride! I ached everywhere! I didn't know so many muscles were needed to stay on a horse's back and point him in the right direction. Food, a jug of wine and I was asleep.

The following morning I was stiff. I wished I had managed to stay awake long enough, the night before, to apply some of my emollients to the tender areas. Still, even at this late stage they helped. Then some food and we were off on the final leg of the journey. I did not enjoy the second day. I ached, I was saddle-sore, I became more aware of the risk of bandit attack and the journey seemed endless. Philip, however, had been alone on that very same road with only his speeding horse for reassurance and company. Both days were, in the event, uncomplicated. Eventually – and to my great relief – the city appeared in the distance. Its walls, the temple visible high above the walls and the noise, as we approached, all identified our destination. There were busy markets outside the city and we met more and more people, herds and flocks – all going in the same direction – as we got closer. We were met, outside the city, by several of the brothers. They took us into the city and told us that this was the gate through which the Lord was taken to Golgotha or Calvaria as it is called in Latin. It was only then that it dawned on me that the low, rounded hill I could see, with two caves towards its base, really did look remarkably like a skull. When I was finally allowed to dismount, we met with Mnason the Cypriot who took us to his house (where Paul was to stay), gave us a tremendous welcome and also spread the word of our arrival to the other disciples in Jerusalem. Oh, but the relief of soft cushions to sit and rest on. That outdid all the celebrations.

Our official welcome, however, was not altogether as we had hoped. There was, obviously, considerable tension or distrust between the Jewish Christians and the Gentile converts. James, the Lord's brother, was now the leader of the Jerusalem group – since Peter was away preaching and evangelising much of the time – and, when we met them, he greeted us warmly, but Paul had hoped for greater enthusiasm with regard to what God had achieved amongst the Gentile converts. It was only when we poured out the collection from the Gentile churches for the poor and needy of the Jewish church, that the atmosphere improved, but there was still an uneasiness. It transpired that the Jewish believers still rigidly adhered to Moses' law and ritual practices and many truly thought that the Gentiles should do so too. James said he had written to them, agreeing many concessions, but also spelling out some things with which they had to conform. James was, clearly, unhappy and suggested (I thought it was more of a command than a request) that Paul should clearly establish his own continuing obedience to the Law by joining in the purification rites of four men who had taken Nazarite vows and also pay their expenses. Paul seemed content to avoid conflict between the two factions of the Faith and agreed to do so. The next day he went with them and purified himself, too – and the ceremony lasted a week.

Then the trouble started. The seven days were barely completed, when Paul was seen in the Temple by some of the Asian Jews. They accused him of bringing Trophimus the Ephesian into the Temple (which he had not done), thereby defiling it and of teaching against the Law and the Jews in general. A riot started – reminiscent of the one in Ephesus. The whole city seemed to descend on the Temple, Paul was dragged out and the gates were slammed shut. It is fortunate that the Roman garrison in the Antonia fortress constantly overlooks the Temple area, expecting trouble; a detachment was sent down, just in time to stop the crowd from beating Paul to death. He was put in chains and was to be taken back to the barracks, when he asked the commander of the guard, in Greek, to be allowed to speak to the crowd. The commander, Tribune Claudius Lysius, was a bit doubtful, at first, but when Paul explained that he was a Jew from Tarsus, in Cilicia, one of the most affluent and great university cities of the world, and not simply a trouble-maker, he was given permission to do so. So he stood on the steps of the Antonia fortress, but spoke in Aramaic – the language of the people. This stopped them in their tracks and they fell silent and listened to him. The commander and the guard obviously did not understand what Paul was saying, but they were impressed by the way he held the attention of the crowd. He gave a brief history of his Pharisaical family, his origins, education, training in the Law of the Fathers of their nation – under the tuition of Gamaliel, who was the most eminent teacher of the time – of his zeal in the persecution of those who offended against Judaism, and of his conversion experience on the Damascus road, when he was in pursuit of the followers of The Way. He described his time with Ananias and the message from God that he was given, both then and later in a vision or trance – in that very Temple – that he was to go to the Gentiles and convert them. That did it! Converting Gentiles into Jews was fine, but converting them into followers of The Way without making them Jews first was totally unacceptable. They went wild! I was standing on the steps, a little distance from Paul, and I was almost crushed by the angry mob trying to reach him to tear him apart! The guard forced the mob back and the commander had Paul taken into the barracks. We, later, discovered that he had had Paul put in heavy chains and was about to have him flogged for causing trouble, when Paul let the centurion in charge know that he was a

Roman citizen. As if the commander had not had enough trouble! It was bad enough to have him chained, but it would have been a very serious offence for a Roman citizen to be subjected to a military flogging without trial. Paul gave his solemn guarantee that he was born a Roman citizen in Tarsus – and the commander ruefully commented that he had had to pay dearly for his own status. Paul was released from the chains, but was detained overnight.

The next day, the commander summoned the Sanhedrin to convene and brought Paul before them, to see if he could determine the Jews' complaint against him. There was tension from the word go! Paul seems to have started off on the wrong foot because of his deteriorating sight. He didn't recognise the high priest – all he could see was a figure in white and called him a 'whitewashed wall'! Insults then seem to have been thrown between both parties, but Paul capitalised on the presence of both Pharisees and Sadducees by saying that he was only on trial before them because of his hope in the resurrection of the dead. The expected violent row ensued between the two factions of the Sanhedrin, since the Sadducees do not believe in the resurrection. The Pharisee teachers ended up supporting one of their own saying they found no fault in Paul, but such was the uproar that the guard was again needed to extricate him and take him back to the barracks.

I presume the next phase of the story depended entirely on Paul's Pharisaical family background, though I never did manage to find out how, for certain. Paul's sister discovered that a plot had been hatched between some men and some of the chief priests and elders, to get Paul brought across the city on the pretext of getting more information about his case. In the narrow streets the guard would have had difficulty in protecting their prisoner from an armed band of determined assassins – and that would have been the end of Paul, and their troubles. Since Paul was detained under guard rather than imprisoned, she was sure her young son would be able to get into the barracks to see him, if he took along a basket of food and wine – especially if there was some wine for the guard! He was admitted and told Uncle Paul what was afoot. The centurion was called; the lad was taken to the commander and related all to him. By now, the commander had had enough. There was to be no mistake, this time: Paul would have to leave the district. Two centurions were summoned to arrange a large detachment of two hundred soldiers, seventy horsemen and packhorses together with mounts for Paul so that he could be taken safely, that night, to Caesarea the provincial capital, to the care of Procurator Felix. Since, as I've said, the journey is about 65 milia, we later learned from Paul that when they got to Antipatris and were safely away from potential trouble, they rested. The next day the foot soldiers returned to the Antonia barracks and Paul went on with the cavalry. When they arrived at Caesarea, Paul was presented to Procurator Felix, together with a letter from Claudius Lysias, which Felix formally read out to Paul and those present, explaining the tribune's action, and stating that he had ordered Paul's accusers to attend on the Procurator to state their case. So Paul was kept, under guard, in Herod's palace to await the arrival of his accusers, who then had to journey from Jerusalem. He did not know it then, but he was to be detained under guard in Caesarea for two years.

We knew little of this for well over a week. One of the brothers went to the barracks the day after his arrest and was told that Paul had faced the Sanhedrin, but was given no other information and told not to come back. I had put up at an inn nearby, but felt that if too many people enquired too often as to what was happening to Paul, it might make it worse for him – since he had obviously been the cause of much trouble to the commander. Paul's sister had contacted Mnason, as soon as she felt it would be safe to do so, to let him know all that had happened in relation to the plot. Now as Paul had been staying with him from the time of his arrival in Jerusalem, Mnason thought he had sufficient excuse to go to the Antonia fortress to ask the commander what was happening to Paul. He was told that Paul was now imprisoned in Caesarea under the jurisdiction of the Procurator. The word spread around the brothers like lightning, but no-one knew what should be done. I asked Mnason to take me to see Paul's sister, since she seemed to know something of the military protocol, and she told me about the plot, her son getting in to the barracks and of what he had said to the centurion and commander. It was reasonable, therefore, to assume that if he was merely detained by the authorities, it might be possible for me to gain access to him as his medical advisor – if I could get to Caesarea. The brothers thought this was an excellent idea, but I thought of the trek on horseback again, and I did not relish the journey on my own!

With a slightly heavy heart I went to the livery stables, recommended by Mnason, to hire a horse; I discovered that there was another small party planning to travel the same route two days later and there was little doubt that they would be happy to let me join them. Since there was no urgency, I made contact with the leader of their group; he was content to let me go along with them, we agreed a meeting place and time and all was set. Lone travellers are always at risk, so it is common practice for individuals to join an organised travelling group – as Philip had done, for the short time he was with the Ethiopian eunuch. I cannot say I enjoyed the journey any more the second time than I had the first, but it was interesting to find we stopped at the same inn, at Antipatris, as Paul and his escort had.

In Caesarea, at least, I had a contact – Philip – so I went straight to his home to seek advice as to where I could find lodging for an uncertain length of time. I was, of course, put up by Philip, who insisted that I should make his home my base, for as long as I was in the district. We talked of the riot in the Temple, the arrest, what might have transpired when Paul faced the Sanhedrin and of the massive escort used to get him out of Jerusalem. Philip was horrified to hear of what had occurred and even more so when we thought of what might have happened! We arranged that we would try to get in to see Paul the following day. I explained to the centurion in charge, that Paul had medical problems that required supervision, I was his personal physician, and that we had travelled from Jerusalem as soon as we had discovered where he had been taken. We were allowed in without undue difficulty. Paul told us of all his recent experiences and, generally, seemed no worse for the ordeal. His frustration was that he did not know what to expect next, nor how long it would all take. When we returned to Philip's home, we talked at length over the evening meal and he suggested that I might be interested in meeting some of his friends and others who had known Jesus. I thought this was an excellent idea and mused on the number of people I might meet who could tell me about the Lord himself, from their own knowledge. For the next few days, Philip was busy with prior commitments, but said that after that, he would be able to accompany me to Galilee; his youngest daughter suggested that we might occupy our time looking around the local countryside, since I could ride. She nearly fell off her horse with laughter when she saw me astride my mount! She could ride as well as her father, so I was treated to riding lessons and I must say that she changed my attitude to riding dramatically. I began to enjoy the ability and confidence of managing a horse. I did not get anywhere near the discomfort I had experienced riding from Caesarea to Jerusalem and back and even quite looked forward to riding with Philip. She took me to visit a few friends in Caesarea, but Jesus had spent most of his time in Galilee, so there would be far more people to meet there.

Philip thought that the first person on our visiting list should be Mary, Jesus' mother. She was staying in Nazareth again, with one of her daughters whose own husband had been unwell. She was now well into her seventies and lived, usually, with her nephew John's family, in Capernaum and had done so ever since Jesus had asked him to care for her, just before he died. We set off in company with a group who were going on to Caesarea Philippi, along the main Roman road – the extension of the Via Maritime – and left them, near our destination, to look for Mary's daughter's home. What a remarkable woman Mary was! Despite hardship and tragedy in her earlier life and regardless of the impositions of advancing years, she retained a dignity and bearing and a clarity of mind that I have rarely seen, either in my professional practice or in my travels. Philip introduced me and explained about Paul. I had so much I wanted to ask her, but one cannot just launch into questioning when one has only just met, about a first-born son, ruthlessly and unjustifiably killed, even after the passage of so many years. We therefore talked politely, discussed my profession, the reasons for my travelling with Paul and so forth, but conversation was very much superficial. We needed to find accommodation for the night, so Philip politely made our excuses to leave and asked that we might visit again the following day. Mary was agreeable to our meeting again the next afternoon, so we left. Next morning, Philip said he was sure that Mary would talk to me more readily if I were on my own, more in a 'doctor–patient' fashion, so he found some 'essential business' in the nearby town of Nain and left us to talk together.

It did not take us long to establish a relationship; Mary relaxed and began to reminisce. She told me of her betrothal to Joseph – who was older than she was – and of the appearance of the angel and how frightened she was. She couldn't understand how she was to be pregnant before she and Joseph were married and she knew that he wouldn't believe the story of an angel! But then, the excitement of knowing she was to be the mother of the Messiah, the Expected One that the prophets had foretold! Joseph and she were both of the House of David, but of different branches. It fitted! She burst out into uncontrollable song. She was also told that her elderly aunt Elizabeth was also pregnant! She had to go to see her! When she got there, she found old aunt Liza beaming happily, already more than six months pregnant, quite convinced that Mary's child would be the Lord and her own would be 'the prophet'. (I thought I might go to the south, to the Judean hill country, to find relatives of her aunt, but Mary said that she and her husband Zechariah were dead. Jesus had said their son John was the prophet of the scriptures, but he was beheaded by Herod and there were no other relatives there, now.)

But what was Joseph going to say about a baby? She had to tell him! He didn't believe her, at first, but then the angel went to see him too and he accepted it all. She told me of the journey to Bethlehem, when she was in late pregnancy, of arriving there in labour. They hoped to stay at an inn, because of the implicit shame of pregnancy before their formal marriage ceremony, but all were full. They had wanted to avoid staying with family, which was the normal thing to do, but they had no alternative anyway. Even then, everyone already had someone staying with them. A distant relative found a space for them, but it was the part of the house where the animals were kept! Her son was born there, amongst the animals, and laid to rest on a bed of hay, in a manger. Hardly had she been tidied up and her baby put to the breast after the birth, when in came a group of shepherds, excitedly telling of bright lights in the sky, angels singing, and of being told to go and look for the new-born baby who was to be the Saviour of their nation. She told me of the presentation of their son at the Temple in Jerusalem at his circumcision, and of Simeon and Anna, who knew instantly that they were looking at their Lord. After all this they moved into a little house, planning to stay in Bethlehem for a while before returning to their home in Nazareth. They had settled in and had resumed normal family life when the unexpected happened. Early one morning three strangers arrived looking for a young child. Some neighbours had directed them to their home and when they saw Mary's young son, they knelt down before him! 'They were obviously not of our class', said Mary, 'being dressed in elaborate clothing, wearing gold ornaments and seeming positively regal'. They said they had travelled a long way to find him as they had seen his portents in the sky, west of their homeland. He was to be a king, they said, and gave him three little caskets containing gold, frankincense and myrrh. Not long after the strangers left, Joseph had told her they had to go to Egypt and it was difficult to carry the little caskets, together with young Jesus and essential belongings on their donkey.

At this stage, Mary broke off to get some food she had prepared for us. She brought out bread, wine, cheese and fresh fruit and we enjoyed the simple fare and talked of domestic things and of the little town of Nazareth for a while, before she resumed the family narrative for me.

She and Joseph went to Jerusalem every year at Passover time; Jesus went with them the year before his bar-mitzvah – and they lost him! They had travelled a day's journey back towards Nazareth before they missed him. Panic! They had thought he was with the other young boys of the family, in their party, but then they had to go back to find him. Find him they did – in the Temple, talking to the priests and rabbis, who were obviously impressed, not only by his knowledge, but also boundless curiosity! By this time, Mary had had three more sons and a daughter and, later, had another son and two more daughters, the youngest – a girl – being fourteen years younger than Jesus. Joseph was a cabinetmaker – and a good one too – and he taught Jesus his trade. Jesus learned well, which was fortunate because, when he was about sixteen years old, Joseph fell ill and was not able to do much work; he died two years later, when the youngest girl was only four years old and, as eldest son, Jesus was expected to maintain the family.   He, too, was good and taught his brothers and the family firm developed a good reputation in the district. It did mean, however, that he was responsible for the family until his youngest sister was betrothed. Then, aged thirty, he left home, leaving his brothers to care for Mary. He first went south, to Bethany-beyond-Jordan, not very far from the family home of Mary's aunt Elizabeth, where his cousin John was preaching and baptising.   John, apparently, told Mary – when he saw her some time later – that he realised that Jesus was the Expected One, but Jesus still insisted on being baptised. When he went down into the water, with John, they all heard a thunderous noise, like a voice from heaven, saying 'This is my son' and a dove flew down and settled on Jesus' shoulder.

After this, Jesus spent some time on his own, in the Judean wilderness before coming back to Nazareth. He did not return to the family business, as they had all expected, but went about the countryside preaching and teaching. Mary told me that on one occasion, at the synagogue in Nazareth, some nine months or so after he first left home, Jesus had taken the scroll for the reading and after reading the passage from Isaiah, where it says, 'the Spirit of the Lord is upon me', he sat down to teach. He taught with clarity and authority, as though the reading referred to himself. The people were impressed, at first, but then began to get offended because he was presuming too much and he was only Joseph's son! Even his brothers were embarrassed – and Mary admitted that she was, too. This prompted Jesus to leave Nazareth, so he taught around Galilee, living mostly at Capernaum. He never did return to Nazareth, though Mary saw him from time to time in Capernaum when she went to visit her sister Salome and her family who had a home there. She told me of his reputation for preaching and healing and of other miraculous happenings. She told of the way he offended the scribes, Pharisees and teachers of the Law, until they could stand it no longer and had him arrested. Roman law allowed the Jews to control the population with their own law, but did not permit them to exact the death penalty by crucifixion. Somehow, they had persuaded Pilate, the procurator, that Jesus was a risk to Rome and he was crucified. Simeon – all those years ago – had told her that she would suffer because of her son; to see him hanging on a Roman cross, dying, nearly killed her too. It was only because John – her sister Salome's son – took her to his home, away from the execution, that she managed to survive. Quiet, comfort and wine with a few drops of tincture of mandragora, helped her recover her composure. (Which reminds me that I must correct an error. I have read John Mark's writing in which he suggests that Jesus had been given wine with myrrh, on the cross – an understandable mistake for someone who is unacquainted with medicine. It was not myrrh – a stimulant – but mandragora, which is sedative. The amount in morion[3] – the solution of mandragora in wine given to victims of crucifixion – is considerably greater than the few drops of tincture we use for patient sedation.) Mary had wanted to go to the tomb, with the others to complete the ritual preparation of his body, after the Sabbath, but Salome wouldn't hear of it. When she came back, breathless, saying the tomb was open, the body wasn't there and an angel had said Jesus had risen from the dead, Mary did not believe her sister! She had, however, been present, with others, when Jesus had re-appeared, but although she had hoped, he never appeared to her alone. Mary lived with John and his family after the crucifixion, but now he was travelling and preaching and was, presently, in Ephesus. He had wanted her to go with him, but she preferred stay with her sister, John's mother; she had, however, come back to Nazareth for a while so that she could be with her youngest daughter until her husband had recovered. Perhaps she would go to Ephesus with John, after the troubles had resolved.

Time had flown! We had been talking for hours. Mary invited me to stay for an evening meal, but I felt that I had taken up too much of her time. I thanked her for talking to me and giving me such valuable background information, made my apologies and left. I walked slowly back to the inn we had stayed at the night before, turning over all that Mary had said, in

---

[3] Morion was known as 'death wine'. It was a strong solution of mandragora (mandrake) in wine which induced a death-like state: cold, pallid skin, imperceptible breathing and no palpable heart-beat (as Friar Lawrence explains to Juliet in Act IV Scene 1 of Romeo and Juliet by William Shakespeare).

my mind. If Philip was to take me to see all the people he had promised, I would have many scrolls of notes! I sat, with a jug of wine, waiting for Philip to return. I had made detailed notes on my travels with Paul and of his teaching, whilst we were in Corinth; I had spent much of the time at sea logging our experiences from the time we left Corinth to shortly before our arrival at Ptolemais – and the more recent occurrences were still very fresh in my mind. I was still pondering on this when Philip returned; I was so deep in thought that I had not noticed him until he sat down beside me. It was too late to go back to Caesarea that night, so we planned to have a meal, stay at the inn, and return the following day. Philip is easy to talk with and we discussed my visit to Mary and my musings as I had walked back from her daughter's home. Philip then threw out a challenge that I had not been expecting. He said that Paul had written a number of letters to the young churches – teaching, admonishing, encouraging. John Mark and others had written, too, but if he could arrange for me to meet and talk to Peter and James, as well as some of the other disciples and friends, then I could write the story of Our Lord's life, his teaching about the Kingdom of God, the significance of his crucifixion and resurrection, and of the beginnings of The Way. It would be helpful for the evangelists to have a written story when they spoke to Gentiles, especially if it was chronological, well written and – by a Gentile. I was stunned, to say the least! I enjoy writing and like to be logical and organised in my thought, but I am a doctor – am I able to be a historian as well? I had travelled to Troas with a medical interest, but I had accompanied Paul because of my interest in and fascination by the growing Faith and the dedication of those who were involved. I had no immediate answer to Philip's challenge: it would require considerable thought and prayer before making such a commitment and I would not take it on unless I could reasonably expect to succeed with such a task. We retired for the night, but I had little sleep. The immensity of the task was only exceeded by the enormity of the responsibility associated with it. I would need to meet not only Peter and James, but as many people as possible who were acquainted with the Lord – those who were not committed to him, as well as his followers. The next morning, tired and rather more silent than usual, I rode back to Caesarea with Philip.

Over the course of the next week or so, Philip made occasional tentative enquiries as to whether I had had further thoughts on the matter, but then, one evening, took the initiative by telling me that both Peter and James were in Jerusalem and we were going to see them. Thereafter he seemed to consider the matter settled – I was going to write the story and that was that! I now needed to meet all who had information – and we were starting with the leaders.

You will recall that I had seen James when we took the collection to Jerusalem with Paul and the others, but the meeting was between Paul and James and I really didn't have chance to say much. This time James agreed to meet me and talked, not only about the church, but also about the Lord (his brother) and the family and all the problems they had during the years of Jesus' ministry. The family difficulties when their elder brother left the family business and responsibilities to them. The embarrassment of having a brother who was constantly at logger-heads with the authorities. The disbelief when followers seemed to be saying, blasphemously, that their brother Jesus was 'the One who was to come'! He told me of the family's outrage, when they tried to see him, one day when he was teaching, only to hear that he called all those around 'his mother and his brothers'. We talked at great length about the spread of the Faith after the resurrection, the conflict between the Jews, the Jewish Christians (as they were now called) and the Gentile converts. Time passed quickly as James talked to me. I thanked him for seeing me and for all the information he had given, and arranged to meet Peter the following morning.

Peter was a totally different character! He was known, by the others on the Lake, as the Big Fisherman, with every justification. He stood a head taller than all of them and he was powerfully built, but he was a gentle character and full of humility. He told me that this had not always been so; when he and Andrew had joined the Zebedees, he had been strong-willed, opinionated, somewhat cynical and even aggressive if someone crossed him! He had changed during the time he had been with Jesus, but even more so after he had been humiliated at the time of Jesus' death. He had bragged that he would follow Jesus to the end, even if it meant dying in the process – and then he denied even knowing him, in the high priest's courtyard! He told me of many strange experiences: taking an enormous haul of fish one morning, after working all night and getting nothing – just because Jesus had told him to cast the net again. He told me of many other 'miraculous' happenings: how Jesus cured his mother-in-law when she had a fever, fed 5000 people with next to nothing, walked on the water, healed the sick and raised the dead. I thought I should try to see some of these people if they were still alive and in the vicinity. Malchus, Peter told me, was still living near Jerusalem – he had had his ear cut off by Peter at the time of the arrest in Gethsemane and Jesus had stuck it on again! He told me about the time when he was boasting about seniority in the group and Jesus gently explained to him the risks of being tempted to think he was better, or more senior, than the others. Jesus had told him that he, too, knew about such temptation – he had been tempted in the desert, right at the start of his ministry. He told me about the arrest, the trial and Jesus' resurrection; how he and John had run to Joseph's garden, when Mary of Magdala came and told them the tomb was empty. He talked of the appearances, the ascension, Pentecost, and the Holy Spirit. I am sure Peter could have talked non-stop for days on end; we talked all morning, had a meal together, talked all afternoon, ate dinner, and I had to drag myself away or I would never have had a night's sleep!

The following day Philip left me to go to Azotus and I tracked down Malchus. He had been the high priest's servant at the time of Jesus' arrest, but now, in his early sixties, he was in charge of the entire administrative staff of the high priest's palace. I had no appointment, but I asked to see Malchus as a physician visiting Jerusalem, about a matter in which only he would be able to help. He was obviously curious and agreed to see me. I explained that I was interested in unusual healings and told him what I had heard about his injury. He seemed content to talk to me and showed no ill feeling toward Jesus – nor great sorrow with regard to the manner of his arrest and death – but he was pleased with the result of his head injury. He confirmed what Peter had said, but when I examined his ear, there was no sign of scarring; the ear was perfectly normal and I could never have detected, by examination, the fact that it had been completely severed!

Having been fired by finding Malchus, I next thought that it might be sensible to try to seek out others who had been healed or at least someone who knew them well enough to give me medical information. Whilst in the vicinity of Jerusalem, I should be able to find Lazarus and, perhaps, someone who knew of the crippled woman whom Jesus had healed. I left Jerusalem and headed out to Bethany. Lazarus was not difficult to locate; I only had to stop at the village store and ask and three people told me that he now lived alone, just at the edge of the village. His sisters still lived together in the old family home and he visited them frequently, but he preferred to be on his own. I easily found his house, but he was not there. I tethered my horse and sat in the shade of a big sycamore-fig tree and waited. It was hot and apart from the murmuring buzz of insects, there was little noise. I dozed. I was suddenly woken by a tall, quietly spoken, weather-beaten fellow in his late fifties, asking why I was asleep outside his door. I tried to gather my sleepy thoughts and said I was looking for Lazarus, the brother of Mary and Martha. 'So you've found him', he said, 'and what can he do for you?' Have you ever been in that situation? My prepared questions and organised thoughts were lost! To give myself time to think, I introduced myself, explained why I had been in Jerusalem — and gradually recovered my composure. I told Lazarus that I was particularly interested in Jesus' healings and since all knew of Jesus calling him from the grave, I hoped he would be kind enough to tell me something about it.

Whereas Malchus was only too ready to discuss his case with me, Lazarus was withdrawn and reluctant. He said he remembered being ill and his sisters being worried about him, but then he thought he went to sleep. The next thing he could recall was hearing Jesus' voice calling and finding that he was bound up and in the dark. He had struggled and freed himself sufficiently to go towards the voice and then found that he had been in a tomb. No, he didn't want to tell me anything more; there wasn't anything more to say, anyway. He said I could always talk to his sisters, if I wished, but didn't think I would learn much more. I changed the subject and asked if he knew of the crippled woman Jesus had cured. He relaxed and talked about the day it happened, but it was much further north, towards Galilee and she had died a few years ago. She had two sons who were – he thought – still living near the family home. He was sure that if I went on to Jericho and then followed the river Jordan for about ten or eleven milia, to the point where a small river joined it, I would find their village. I thanked him and left.

I did call in on the sisters on the way back to Jerusalem and they chatted a lot about Jesus and the Twelve, but they could add nothing to what Lazarus had told me; he had always refused to discuss the missing four days of his life. I wondered whether, if I went to Nain, I would manage to get the widow's son to talk – but in the event, when I did eventually find him at Nain some three or four weeks later, I learned no more from him than I had from Lazarus!

I needed to leave messages for Philip as to what I was doing and to let him know that I would make my own way back to Caesarea, so I put up at an inn for the night and rode out on the Jericho road the next day. No, I did not travel alone. That really is a dangerous road and always has been. But it was not difficult to locate the village and find Jacob, one of the sons. He told me that in her younger days, his mother was fit, busy and stood straight, but when he was about sixteen, she had complained of back and neck pain and gradually she became bent and completely unable to stand up straight. Latterly, she had walked with difficulty and could not look ahead much further than her feet. She had been like this for about eighteen years, but Jesus cured her instantly! She had straightened up, her pain went and she had no further trouble to the day of her death. The diagnosis was obvious: she had had degenerative ankylosis of the spine – for which there is no known cure! I was increasingly impressed by the Lord's ability to cure the incurable – even to 'cure' death!

Whilst in this region, my next thought was to find people who could tell me about the Lord. I went back to Jericho and found Zacchaeus and his family: he was a fascinating character who explained many of the intricacies of the tax system and what he had been and done in the past. He even told me how he had put himself at risk of ridicule when he had climbed a sycomore-fig tree to see Jesus; as a senior and affluent man in Jericho, climbing trees was not something expected of him. He had been determined to see Jesus and because he was short of stature, he could not see over the heads of the crowd. Jesus had come to his home that evening, and eaten with his family, and had totally changed his way of life as a result! I spoke to many others, too, who told me how they had met Jesus and what effect he had had on them. I found Timaeus' son – now a very old man – who had been born blind, but had been given sight by Jesus. He still seemed to be amazed by the fact that he could see, whereas we, who have sight, take that gift for granted! I also needed to go to Jerusalem to find the garden of Joseph of Arimathea (it would have been good to talk to him – but he had died years ago) and to go to Temple, the Mount of Olives and Gethsemane.

Gethsemane! What a place! Quiet, peaceful and one could imagine being there with the Lord, but for as long as it exists it will epitomise the complex association of the Lord in prayer, and his arrest at Passover. In Jerusalem itself, many were prepared to give me personal stories, which helped to fill in background. To one I am particularly grateful; he said I should go to Emmaus, where Cleopas' eldest son still lived. He would be able to give me a story well worth recording. He said it would not take long to get there on horseback, as it was only about seven milia from the Temple in Jerusalem, going westwards. He was right! Ishmael was only too pleased to tell me how his father and uncle had been walking home from the city, on the first day of the week after Jesus had been crucified, when a stranger joined them on the Joppa road, just beyond the city wall. They were discussing all that had happened over the past three days and he came along and joined in their conversation. He went through the scriptures with them, and though they were depressed about the arrest and death of Jesus, he explained that this was already written about. It had to happen to the Christ. His father brought the stranger in to have a meal with them and to stay the night, as it was late. It was then that young Ishmael met him. He said they all sat down to eat; the stranger said the prayers that his father should have said, broke bread and then disappeared! He said the 'grown-ups' then realised that they had been in the presence of the risen Jesus. They got up from the meal and ran back to Jerusalem to tell all the disciples! I stayed, in all, about three weeks and then joined a caravan, slowly going north, through Samaria to Ptolemais. This gave me the chance to talk to Samaritans and, particularly to see Jacob's well in Sychar. I left the caravan in Samaria itself and joined, successively, with several groups going westwards, and returned to Philip's home in Caesarea.

I was glad to be back: Philip and I talked late into the night. He was anxious to know what I had learned and whom I had met, where I had been and what I had seen. He was pleased with my 'report', but said I should now go back to Galilee, where there would be so many more contacts to make, since Jesus had lived and taught more in Galilee than anywhere else. I needed to see Paul, too, as I had been away for quite a long time.

It was several days later that I managed to get in to see Paul again. He was fascinated and delighted with Philip's idea of my writing a history of the Lord and The Way. He was impressed with the amount of information I had already collected on my travels and encouraged me to go to Galilee to meet more people who had met Jesus. Although free access was allowed to his friends and other visitors, Paul was beginning to get frustrated with his detention, but had been intrigued by the interest Felix and his wife (a Jewess) had shown in The Way and his involvement with it. They had repeatedly sent for him, to talk to them – but he had a suspicion that there may have been an implied preparedness to let him go free, if he were to offer them a bribe. His principles would not have allowed this and he remained resigned to a future of house arrest.

Paul's continued detention did allow me to tour Galilee, as suggested by Philip, and meet many more people who had met and known the Lord. By then I had three scrolls of notes, disjointed stories and references that would require considerable reorganisation into a logical, readable presentation if I was to meet the expectations of Philip's challenge. So many people had been anxious to tell me of their experiences of the Lord's journeys, his teaching, his healings and his personality – but it was all some twenty-five to thirty years ago. I would never be able to determine the exact sequence of all these events. Where this task proved to be patently impossible, I thought perhaps it would be better to relate stories in proximity to emphasise teaching points.

Some two years or so after Paul had first arrived in Caesarea, Procurator Felix was replaced by Porcius Festus. Having kept him under house arrest for two years, Felix should (according to Roman law) have released Paul, but – since he seemed to want to favour the Jews – Felix left him to the mercies of Festus.

Three days after he was installed in post, in Caesarea, Festus went up to Jerusalem. The chief priests and leaders lost no time in presenting themselves to him and tried to persuade him to send Paul back to Jerusalem to face their charges again, but Festus told them that Felix had had sufficient trouble with them and Paul, and if they wished to raise the case again they would have travel to Caesarea with their lawyers and formally present their challenges in his court in Caesarea. They did, but could prove nothing; Festus still suggested that Paul might agree to go to Jerusalem and face trial there. Paul was adamant: he had done nothing wrong, neither to the Jews nor against Rome. He, therefore, claimed his right to take his case to Caesar. Festus accepted this, but before it could be arranged King Agrippa and Bernice, his wife, arrived to see the new procurator and Festus took this opportunity to relate the difficulties and get Paul to present his case once again, before an acknowledged authority on Jewish Law. I was present, this time when, for a fifth time, Paul was required to relate his story – to defend himself. Each time he had done so, he biased the background of events to the interests and standpoint of his audience, whether the Jews at the Temple, the Sanhedrin, the procurators or Agrippa himself. Neither of the procurators nor King Agrippa had found Paul guilty of anything which required the death penalty, nor even continued imprisonment, but since he had appealed to Rome, Festus had every intention of sending him there – out of harm's way! Paul seemed content; he expected a fair hearing, freedom, and he would be where his longing was driving him. Rome!

That was a journey I shall never forget! Julius, a centurion of the Imperial Regiment, was charged with escorting prisoners to Rome – we were to go under his command and we were all classified as prisoners too. Paul was still, effectively, under house arrest, but Aristarchus (a fellow Macedonian) and I seemed to have been listed as Paul's slaves! The centurion commandeered a ship from Adramyttium, which was plying the coast of Asia Minor and now returning to its home port, and we were all taken aboard. We were given some privileges, however.

When we reached Sidon, we were all permitted to go ashore to see the brothers there and stay with them overnight. We didn't get much sleep; Paul talked late into the night, relating what had happened to him over the past two years and more, explaining why we were going to Rome and encouraging them in the faith. He never ceases to amaze me! Despite a recurring fever and the continuing trouble with his eyes, the amount of writing or teaching he undertakes, or whatever else occupies his time, he seems to need very little sleep. We were up early the next morning and Paul seemed fresher than any of us. Back on board, sails set and we were under way towards Myra – a long and tedious journey as we put in at all the little ports all the way up the coast. When at last we disembarked at Myra, the centurion next commandeered an Alexandrian grain ship, which was taking her cargo to Rome; now, we had a much larger vessel with huge sails, so the expectation was that we should make faster and more reliable progress. If only!

We struck out westward from Myra towards Cnidos – the furthermost point of Asia Minor – intending to moor in the commercial harbour, which was adjacent to the military trireme harbour, but south-facing and sheltered. We would need to take on stores, and the ship's owner intended stocking up with some of the local wine that was much favoured in Rome. The offshore wind was stronger than we had expected and the downdraught, as it came between the mountains was fierce! Not only that, but as it hit the open sea, it effectively changed direction. The result was similar to sailing between islands (as I have explained before – but more so), so the sailors not only had the strength of the wind to contend with, but also had to try to keep the sails appropriately set. The result was that we could only have the bare essentials of sail up and made slow progress in our intended direction. Having passed between the mainland and Rhodes, we became aware that we had no hope of making Cnidos and were being driven further southwest towards Crete. We found harbour at Fair Havens and anchored up for a day. The wind then abated somewhat and there began an argument between Paul, the ship's owner and its captain. Paul had considerable experience of the Great Sea and said that it would be dangerous to go on, even if Fair Havens was not a good overwintering port. The owner wanted to get to Rome and would not be tied to this small port for the winter, but grudgingly agreed that we might try to reach Phineka, further to the west and ride out the storm there. The wind had different ideas! We had not long slipped our moorings when the wind picked up to hurricane force. This northeaster blew us further to the southwest, well away from Crete and it was only the brief respite of the lee of the island of Cauda that allowed us to haul the water-logged ship's longboat aboard. The storm was fierce and we feared that the ship might break up; she was a coastal craft and wasn't built for such weather. Her hull was long and not rigid, and there was the risk that when cresting a wave, she could break her back. We put ropes around the hull, both fore and aft, to hold the timbers together and then lashed these 'frappings' to the mast, together with other stays from the stern and bow, to try to stop her hull from flexing with the waves. Throughout, we knew that somewhere to the south there were the notorious sand bars of Syrtis, which would be the certain death of us all, were we to hit them! The mainsail was more danger than benefit: we lowered it and cast out the sea anchor to slow the ship. We knew not where we were. We could do no more than run with the storm, with our little sprit-sail to keep our head up. We saw no sun and few stars; one brief glimpse did show us that the wind had veered and we were running westward – at least there was less chance of running onto the sand bars. Over the next few days the storm was terrifying! The ship wallowed before the wind, so to lighten her we threw much of the extra cargo overboard and all the spare tackle. We could do little about the grain; although the sacks were heavy, at least they were packed tightly and would therefore not shift and cause us to list. That would have been very quickly fatal! Day followed night and night followed day and the weather did not ease at all. There were 276 men on board, all worried, many seasick and nobody could contemplate eating. Another full week passed and we were beginning to lose heart, but on the morning of the tenth day out from Crete, Paul got the company together. He told them that they should have taken his advice and stayed at Fair Havens, but nevertheless, an angel from God had appeared to him during the night and assured him that no one would be lost – only the ship. He told me that the angel had said that this was to be, because he had to appear for trial before Caesar. Four more days passed, without change in the weather and we drifted helplessly westward, before the wind, across the Adriatic Sea.

I am not a professional seaman and therefore do not understand how the next warnings were initiated, but it seemed very like intuition to me About midnight, one of the senior seamen called for the lead to sound the depths; he thought there was a risk that we were in shallowing water. The first sounding showed 20 orguias[4]; a short time later, it was only 15 orguias. There was sudden panic! In an attempt to slow our progress, they dropped four sea anchors off the stern. Some of the sailors tried to lower the longboat, saying they were going to drop anchors from the bow too, but it was obvious that they were trying to get away and save themselves and the centurion cut the lines holding the boat and it fell away. Paul then called on all the company to eat some food, as they hadn't eaten for well over a week. He broke bread, gave thanks to God for our lives, ate and the others followed suit. We then set to and threw the sacks of grain overboard to lighten the ship and reduce her draught. At daybreak, the look-out called 'land in sight' and as we were heading towards a sandy bay, the centurion ordered the anchors to be cut free and we ran towards the shore. Unfortunately, we hit a sand-bar and the ship started to break up. Sudden panic – personal panic, this time! I had to get my medicines and scrolls, quite apart from my other belongings. I had taken some oiled linen aboard with me – a wise precaution for a sea journey – and wrapped my precious notes and medicines as securely as I could to protect them from the sea, but the rest of my things were left behind. When I got back on deck, I found the soldiers were going to kill all the prisoners (ourselves included), but the centurion stopped them, ordered all to swim ashore or float in on planks of driftwood, but to abandon ship immediately. I can swim, but I found a plank near me and, to keep my precious cargo as dry

[4] An orguia was a Greek measurement equal to about one fathom (six feet).

as possible, I used it to float and paddle ashore. As Paul had said – no one was lost!

The place where we had landed was called Malta, the largest of a small archipelago of four islands and, despite the weather, it seemed the entire population of the island had gathered on the beach to welcome us. As the wind was cold and it was raining, the first of the ship's company ashore, helped by the islanders, lit a fire on the beach. Paul went collecting firewood, too. Aristarchus and I were horrified, as were the islanders, when a viper came out of the brushwood and struck at Paul's hand. They thought this must be a sign of retribution for his sins, but he shook it off and to the amazement of all – including us – he suffered no ill effects from the viper venom and the locals then hailed him as a god. God really did want him to get to Rome!

The islanders were very friendly and helpful people. The chief official of the island, Publius, had an estate near the bay and welcomed Paul, Aristarchus, Julius our centurion and me to his home and entertained us most nobly for three days, whilst we found longer term accommodation in the town. When we first went to his home, we met Publius' father who was ill with dysentery and had a high fever, but Paul told him not to worry, laid his hands on the old man, prayed and the fever abated almost instantly. When the local populace heard of this, he was required to lay hands on all the sick in the vicinity! Healing by faith was now a natural phenomenon, so far as I was concerned.

We were now committed to staying on Malta for the winter and after those two horrendous weeks at sea, I was glad not to have to think about the sea and ships for a while. That storm continued for almost a week. When it eased, the sky cleared and the winter sun shone again, we could see the smaller islands to the northwest. The islanders told us that the largest of these, Gozo, was inhabited, but the two smaller ones were not. There was a watchtower on the smallest one, but as winter set in, it was left unmanned – the weather kept any potential invaders at bay. I wondered whether we might visit Gozo when the winter was past, but as soon as sailing became possible, the centurion commandeered another Alexandrian ship, which had also overwintered on the island, and we were heading for Rome again. Most of the big ships had carved figureheads, but this was the first I had seen with a double one; it represented the twin gods Castor and Pollux – the patrons of seafarers who, according to their superstitious beliefs, had to care for storm-bound ships. We had certainly fitted that category!

We had overwintered on Malta for three months and had become very friendly with the local people. Paul had taught and converted many and when it came time for us to leave, they gave us all the supplies we needed and there was yet another emotional farewell on the quayside. With a fair wind – and advice from the locals – we headed to the northeast (leaving the little islands of Cominetto, Comino and Gozo unvisited), towards Syracuse in Sicily, where we stayed for three days. Julius obviously had business to complete there; we should have reached the port some three months or so earlier, so some explanations would be required. When all was settled, we set sail for Rhegium, where we took on more stores and fresh water. We were not allowed to stay ashore at Rhegium since our centurion wanted an early start the next morning. At dawn the sails were set and we found we had a favourable southerly wind and simply ran before it. By mid-morning the strength of the wind had increased and I began to wonder whether we were again courting disaster, but the sky remained clear and the wind powerful but steady. We travelled! Such was our speed on the water that we covered about 200 milia by the middle of the next day and put in at Puteoli. This was to be the last port we would see for a long time and when we disembarked we were delighted to find that there were some Christian brothers and sisters there. Since Julius had to await further instructions from Rome, Paul, Aristarchus and I were allowed to stay with these friends. They told us about the brothers in Rome. They had been part of a small group there, but had left to set up business in Puteoli. The Faith was strong, in Rome, but the numbers were few: there was much work to be done to spread the Good News. We stayed with them whilst Julius awaited his orders; they sent word to Rome to say we were on the way to the capital – but it was a week before we started this last lap of the journey. There was, to some extent, the uncertainty of knowing when we would set off, what the overland route would entail and what we would have to face when we reached Rome, but it was good to be again in the company of friends (even if only for a short time) who thought as we did in spiritual matters, who were not driven by military orders, financial ambition or self-gratifying obsession.

The 'road to Rome', however, started with another boat! From Puteoli we embarked on a barge to take us along the canal through the Pontine Marshes to the Forum of Appius – a long, uncomfortable, slow and tedious journey. This was an area, we discovered, which was malodorous and well recognised for its association with the relapsing marsh fever. There were irritating, biting insects flying about and I, for one, was glad when we were back on dry land and far from that unpleasant area. That night we put up at one of the local inns and were delighted to find that more of the brothers from Rome had come along to meet us there. They told us that an even larger crowd had set out from Rome, but most of them had stopped, some ten milia further along the Via Appia, at the town of the Three Taverns. We would meet them the following day and they would escort us back to Rome itself. This did a lot to lift our spirits, as we had all become subject to a mood of discouragement during that journey through the marshes. Paul particularly so, not surprisingly, as he was also apprehensive of what awaited him in Rome. He was enormously encouraged by the Roman brothers; they told him about the Faith in Rome and how all the others were looking forward to seeing him and how honoured they were that he should want to meet them – despite the reasons for his being in Rome and the fact that he was under a Roman guard. We set out next morning and reached the Three Taverns before mid-day. The brothers who had accompanied us were pleased to be away from the Forum of Appius. They didn't like the innkeepers there; they were quite sure they were all dishonest and unreliable. It was for that reason that most of the others from Rome had stopped at the Three Taverns. There was great celebration when we reached that town. We stopped only for refreshment, but for the remaining 35 milia to Rome itself, we had an enthusiastic escort, rejoicing and singing hymns all the way! I was glad Philip's daughter had taught me to ride – the journey was so much more comfortable than when I travelled to Jerusalem.

Rome! Set upon seven hills, the city could be seen long before we got anywhere near it. It was impressive. Rome's warning to potential criminals also impressed us, as we went along the Via Appia, nearing the city – there, stark and horrific were crucified miscreants along the roadside! Roman punishment has always been harsh – the scourge and the cross feature fairly prominently – but it is not vindictive. When no guilt has been found, the prisoner is released – with the notable exception of the Lord – but even then it was Jewish persistence that was responsible. We and our Christian brothers have had far less trouble from Rome than we have from Jerusalem. The Jews have persecuted followers of The Way from the time the Lord first declared, 'The Kingdom of God is at hand'!

We arrived in Rome late in the day: Julius took his prisoners to the prefect of the Praetorian Guard, but we were taken to the head official of the Praetorian Guard who was responsible for prisoners awaiting trial. Paul was accorded custodia militaris, which meant that he was allowed to live in his own rented house, but was chained to a Roman soldier by his right wrist – night and day. Aristarchus and I were allowed to live in the same house, but were given freedom to come and go – as Paul's slaves! We had to wait, now, for a date for his case to be heard by Caesar and for Paul's accusers to arrive from Judea. We had only been in Rome for three days when Paul sent for the Jewish leaders in the city. They came to his house and he launched into an explanation and defence of all that had led to his arrival in Rome.

Much to his surprise, the Jews said that no letters had come from Judea, no visiting Jews had said anything bad about him and they had all heard about this new sect and wanted him to explain the new teaching to them! They arranged a day and many came early in the morning to hear him. In typical fashion, he talked all day. He taught about the coming of God's Kingdom and tried to convince them that Jesus was the Holy One of the scriptures. He began to get difficulty when he told them that salvation is by grace, not by works and the Law, as they had been taught by their rabbis. If they accepted, Jesus' death on the cross paid their penalty, gave them absolution from their sins and eternal life through him. Some believed, but others would not and got up to leave. In frustration, Paul quoted Isaiah at them, about hearing and not hearing; seeing and not seeing. They all left – arguing hotly amongst themselves.

Paul adjusted to the uncertainty of his future, set to work on a program of evangelism and got down to writing letters to his churches. Visitors came and went; Paul preached the Kingdom of God and taught about the Lord – to interested Jews and to Gentiles alike. He returned to his trade of tent-making to raise money to pay for his food and rent and awaited Caesar's pleasure. The Word spread throughout Rome and many, many were converted. Paul did not see much of Rome during these two years, but he saw a lot of Romans. As time went on and no trial was called, he began to hope that no one would come from Judea as witness against him. He used his time profitably in spreading the Word, by direct teaching and by letter to the growing churches and I have had time to organise my notes and thoughts and write, as Philip had suggested. I have completed one scroll already, covering the time from Jesus' birth to his ascension and the second – the spread of the Faith and the growth of the little churches and Paul's work to our arrival in Rome – is approaching completion. If no trial is called, Paul expects to be released and if so, he wants to go to Spain. If he does this, I shall have a third scroll to write!

I have dedicated my present writing to my mentor, Theophilus: he was most generous to me in putting me to study medicine, without which I would not have met Paul, nor would I have had the opportunity to travel and watch the development of The Way worldwide. I am now in a position to offer Theophilus, in return, something more than financial resources: I can offer him the chance of eternal life, securely in the knowledge that my Lord Jesus is undoubtedly the Son of God and is alive in all true believers.

John

The 'Beloved' Disciple

John

The 'Beloved' Disciple

It's a long time, a very long time now, since Jesus walked the hills of Galilee. The others are all dead, long since. I some times feel like Elijah, saying 'I, even I only am left'! Nigh on sixty years have gone by since his dreadful crucifixion, but it all remains as clear now as it ever did. Of the twelve of us, each of the others has died by some dreadful means – Judas, the betrayer, killed himself, but all the others were killed because of what we all believed. Peter and Andrew crucified, my brother James beheaded, others beaten to death. Why have I been spared? Perhaps to tell the story for the new believers – especially our Greek converts! They don't have a Jewish background, but they do have an ability to understand the concept of the Kingdom of God – which is more than can be said for many of our nation! And after all, I knew Jesus longer than the others – he was my cousin. I am well aware that John Mark, who was Peter's disciple, has written about Jesus and what he did, Matthew has written about who Jesus was, and Paul's companion, Luke, has written extensively of Jesus' life, death, and resurrection – as well as making a detailed record of the early church and of those of us who were known as the Apostles. Typical of a doctor, in the way he analysed and documented everything! But they didn't know Jesus as I did!

My mother Salome and Jesus' mother Mary were sisters. My mother was the elder and when she married my father, Zebedee, she left Nazareth and went to live with his family in Capernaum. Father's family was in the fishing business and fairly affluent, owning several boats and employing men from the town. The brothers shared the business, when Grandfather died, but the other brothers had different interests and my father eventually took over all of it. It provided a good income and standard of living for us and when he extended the business to market the catch in Jerusalem, we had to have a house there, as well. We supplied fish to the high priest's palace and Father became very influential in the city. Mother was involved, too. Hebrew women, usually, simply looked after the household and family, but Mother was more like some Roman and Greek women, in that she was involved, did the administration and accounts for the business and, latterly, actually ran it. This gave her an income in her own right – and the ability to supervise the business, which was very useful when James and I were away from home with Jesus. Father had handed the business on to James and me a few years before he died; he kept a continuing interest in fishing and went out in the boats fairly often, but it all got a bit much for him towards the end.

Just a bit further up the coast of Galilee, at Bethsaida, Jonah's sons Simon and Andrew had a fishing boat; one time, when their boat was damaged and sank, Father persuaded them to come into partnership with us as junior partners. They were good fishermen, but they did not have the means to replace their boat and they had been desperately worried as to how they could survive. Timber for boat-building, around Galilee, was so expensive, quite apart from the charges of the boat-builders, themselves.

My Aunt Mary – Jesus' mother – married Joseph when she was about sixteen; he was a lot older than she was and had a thriving workshop in Nazareth. He was a skilled cabinetmaker and ran a carpentry business, providing furniture for most of the up-market families in Nazareth, as well as yokes, ploughs and other farm equipment for the countryfolk. Jesus was about as old as my elder brother James, and he sometimes came to stay with us in Capernaum, when he was young. Nazareth was not a lot of fun for young lads growing up – boats and fishing were. Even when we didn't meet during the year, we always met up at Passover; his family from Nazareth would meet up with ours and we would all travel together to Jerusalem. It was a long journey and, as young lads, we had lots of opportunities for fun on the way.

As time went on, Jesus' father insisted that he should learn his trade, working with wood, so we saw little of him for some while – but he still came to stay when he could. He always said he liked staying with Auntie Sal! Mother liked him, too, and in his later years – when he was teaching and preaching – she provided him with financial support, as though he was her son. His own mother did not have the means to do so and his brothers didn't get on with him, once he became a focus for controversy. It was not until long after Jesus had been crucified and risen again that his brother James accepted that he was the Holy One the scriptures had promised!

James and I were always loud, boisterous, practical fellows: we loved the boats, the nets, the wind and water and enjoyed the family fishing trade. We held strong opinions on things – and voiced them! Jesus called us Boanerges – 'the sons of thunder' – and the name stuck, even in the years when we were his disciples. I remember when we went to a Samaritan village, on the way to Jerusalem for the last time, not long before he died. They didn't want him. Not only that, but they were positively offensive towards him. James and I were furious! We wanted to call down fire from heaven on them, to destroy them and their village – but Jesus told us that we should just quietly ignore them and go on to another more welcoming village. I don't suppose I've changed much over the years, either. Not long ago I was going to the bath-house here in Ephesus, and whilst preparing to bathe I heard the voice of Cerinthus – that heretic leader of the Gnostics[1] – in there as well. I was not going to share a place of cleansing with him! I admit I came storming out, but when my disciples tell the story, they have me running out, only partly clothed, calling on the bath-house to 'fall in on that enemy of truth'! I don't remember that – but perhaps they are right.

Jesus was different from James and me – that is not to say he wasn't a practical character, because Joseph taught him well and he took over their family business when his father died, but he was always quieter and more studious. He was well versed in the scriptures and could not only quote them, but talked about what they meant. He was fun to be with, but

---

[1] A sect who claimed that 'matter is evil and spirit is good'. They therefore held that God could not touch matter and, consequently, could not have created the world.

he could always see more in a situation and beyond it than we could.

Joseph died when Jesus was about eighteen; he had been unwell for a couple of years before that and Jesus had had to take over much of the business of the workshop, whilst his father was still able to give him guidance. It was then up to Jesus to provide for his mother and the family and they were a big family, too – Aunt Mary, five boys and three girls. Mother always used to say that she didn't know how Aunt Mary ever managed to cope with them all. Our mother found it difficult enough to manage just James and me!

In his turn, Jesus had to teach the four younger boys. He was good, too, both practically and in teaching, and his brothers soon learned the trade: they were not as good as Jesus was, however, and although they made a living, the business was never quite the same when they ran it on their own. We didn't see much of him for the three or four years when he was tied to the business, but when his brother James was about eighteen, he sometimes managed to take some time off to visit his Auntie Sal, and he, my brother James and I would go out in the boats, fishing. He seemed to love that: he enjoyed handling the sails, rowing the boat (and she could be very heavy!), hauling in the nets and beaching the boat at the end of the day. He was a powerful fellow and always took his share of the effort; we three got on well together. When the time came for him to return home, he did so cheerfully, but he obviously needed a break from time to time. This lifestyle continued until he was about thirty. Then, with his brothers eminently capable of running the business – and after his youngest sister was betrothed – he felt it was safe to leave the family home in their hands and set out to do what he had planned.

He went south, away down to the Judean hills where our great Aunt Elizabeth and Uncle Zechariah had lived. Our cousin John was born to them when they were both very old. He was about half a year older than Jesus and my brother James, and was a bit like the ancient prophets, living in the desert, preaching 'fire and brimstone', calling all to repentance and baptising. That's why he was known around and about as John the Baptiser. He was in Bethany-beyond-Jordan when Jesus found him.

Andrew and I were disciples of cousin John, by this time. His preaching made sense and he had the fire and enthusiasm that almost demanded that we listen to him. John travelled about, but he was mostly in Judea – though he baptised Andrew and me in the Jordan at Aenon near Salim. Capernaum is quite far in the north; the fishing business made it difficult for us to be with him for long periods of time – particularly when father became incapable of running it on his own – but we got there when we could. In fact, Andrew and I were both with John about the time Jesus came to him at Bethany-beyond-Jordan. Simon had come too, but stayed in the village to complete a contract with the local elders. John told us that the day before we got there, Jesus had come to him for baptism. He had gone down into the water, with John, and after the baptism a dove flew down onto his shoulder. John knew this was to be the sign that this was the 'Son of God'. The people with him said they heard thunder at the same time, but John was sure he had heard the voice of God. It was the next day, when we were with him, that he told us of this and then Jesus came by again and he pointed to Jesus – my cousin – saying this was the 'Lamb of God'! We were stunned! As Jesus walked on his way, we got up and followed him and asked where he was staying, this far south. It was late in the afternoon, but he invited us to go with him; we talked on the way and stayed until late into the evening, discussing the scriptures and Jesus' plans to teach and bring the good news of God's kingdom to the people. He asked us to go with him, as disciples; he seemed to know that John would want us to do so, even without asking. The next day, Jesus planned to return to Nazareth and we went back to John to tell him what had happened. He knew we would want to go with Jesus and was pleased for us. Andrew couldn't wait to tell his brother Simon, all that had gone on; he wanted to convince him that we had seen and met the Messiah! He rushed off to find Simon and took him to meet Jesus. I then left, with all haste, for Capernaum: I needed to tell James and sort out the business, if we were really to have work to do with Jesus! The boats would not sail themselves, the men would not work if they were not instructed and supervised and there was no way we could let the whole set-up, for which we had worked for years, fall to rack and ruin. Father was far too frail, and certainly no longer able to take it over again and manage it.

The next time we saw Jesus was a few weeks later, back in Galilee. Simon and Andrew had been fishing all night and caught little. James and I were preparing our nets to go out later that day and Jesus came along, with a group of men, who were listening to him teaching. Jesus asked if he might borrow Simon's boat, as it was at the water's edge, got into it and talked from there; sound seems to travel better, even across a small stretch of water. It made it easier for the people to see him and hear what he was saying. Having finished teaching, he asked Simon to put the boat out again. Simon was reluctant, because they had fished all night, caught nothing and he was tired, but did as he was asked. He even put out the nets again, when Jesus told him to, although he thought it was a stupid idea – but the catch was tremendous and James and I were needed to help get the haul ashore! Simon was astounded and almost fell at his feet. Jesus simply said to all four of us, that if we followed him, he would make us 'fishers of men'. To Simon, he said that he would be called Peter – 'the Rock' – but this did not make a great deal of sense to us at that time. The encounter did mean that we were all his disciples from then on. Father was left standing in our boat, not quite knowing what was going on. He soon learned!

Whilst we were still in Capernaum, Jesus met Philip, who lived near Simon Peter and Andrew in Beth-saida, and invited him to join the team. Philip was so impressed by Jesus and what he was saying, that he ran to find his friend Nathanael to tell him that he had met Jesus of Nazareth and he was sure that he was 'The One of whom Moses had spoken'. Nathanael, in the usual sceptical Galilean way, said 'nothing good had ever come out of Nazareth and was never likely to' – but he came with Philip and was just as impressed, and joined us to make a company of six.

Now Nathanael came from Cana and just after he had joined us, there was a wedding in his home town. One of our younger cousins was to be married, all the family were invited and Jesus took his new followers – Simon Peter, Andrew, Philip and

Nathanael – along with him. James and I thought this might put a bit of a strain on the family's resources and we were not wrong! Weddings of a virgin are held in the middle of the week; celebrations start in the evening and are expected to last several days – often until the Sabbath. Wine is a vital part of the celebration and although it is a great disgrace to get drunk, it is total humiliation of the family if the wine is of poor quality or if there is insufficient to last the duration of the feast. The master of ceremonies was horrified when the wine ran out. I saw Aunt Mary, looking worried, talking to her younger sister in rather hushed tones and then taking Jesus aside. I heard her tell him that there was no more wine and he said, 'Lady, my time is not yet come, but don't worry. Leave it to me'. He took one of the servants aside and told him to fill the six stone jars with water. That caused no problem as water was needed for ritual hand-washing and for washing feet and each jar held about two and a half metretes[2]. But then you should have seen the expression on the servant's face when Jesus told him to put some in a goblet and take it to the master of ceremonies! He did as he was told, but he was trembling with fear as he gave it to the master to taste. His expression changed from absolute terror to stunned disbelief when 'the wine' was pronounced the best the master had ever tasted. 'Sharon Valley's best', they called it – and they had enough to last that wedding and many other celebrations yet to come. We knew that Jesus was different: we had joined him as disciples because he had something that no one else had. John had called him 'the Lamb of God', we called him 'rabbi', but I

---

[2] A metrete was about 40 litres – i.e. a total of about 600 litres of wine.

did not expect my cousin to work miracles. We had a lot to learn!

It was not long after the wedding that Jesus had invited another four fellows to join his group. Three of them were Zealots – the two Judas's, and Simon who was known as 'The Zealot'. That was a bit risky, I felt, knowing that the Zealots were committed to revolution and organised opposition to Rome. I think they thought, when they first joined us, that Jesus was going to be a leader like Judas Maccabeus of olden times, but they had much to learn, too. When Matthew and his brother James joined, that made our complement up to twelve and that is how we were generally known – 'The Twelve'. Although we were all together, to some extent we were three groups; the Zealots and Matthew's brother had much in common, Jesus, James and I were 'family', but he included Simon Peter with James and me – and he seemed to expect more of us – and then there were the other five. We all spent a lot of time in each other's company, but there were occasions when Jesus took just the three of us with him – particularly when he wanted to be quiet and pray.

We were, then, quite a large group, but we were even larger when Aunt Mary and Jesus' brothers joined us and all stayed with my relatives in Capernaum for a few days, before going up to Jerusalem for our first Passover together. Aunt Mary stayed with Mother, in her room, Jesus and his brothers joined James and me in the big room at the top of the house, some of the others stayed in the cave under the house, others with Peter's family, and the remainder stayed with some of our friends nearby, but all came together, at our home, for meals. The journey to Jerusalem was a bit like old times – all the family travelling together again – but with many new friends as well this time. It was whilst we were in Jerusalem that I remember Jesus having his first major brush with the authorities in the city. He challenged the right to sell and exchange coinage in the Temple courts. They demanded a sign from him to establish his authority for the challenge. It was at that point that he first alluded to the fact that no grave would hold him for long. Neither they nor we understood him. He had said, 'Destroy this temple and I will raise it again in three days'. We all thought he meant Herod's Temple – which had taken forty-six years to build – but he meant that if he were killed, his body would not be in a grave for more than three days.

Many people were impressed by Jesus – with his teaching and by what he was doing in and around Jerusalem (including Nicodemus who was one of the Jewish ruling Council!); they came to him asking for baptism, whilst John was baptising much further to the north at Aenon near Salim. The Authorities had grudgingly accepted John baptising, but when they discovered that even more people were coming to Jesus than going to John (though we were actually doing the baptisms, not Jesus himself) they were furious! There was an obvious threat to his ministry and to the safety of all of us, so Jesus decided to leave Jerusalem and get back to Nazareth in Galilee as quickly and as safely as possible. Going through the hill country of Samaria was the shortest distance, but not the easiest route – but the Jews were not likely to follow us into Samaritan territory. We had travelled about 30 milia when we came to Jacob's well, near Sychar at the foot of Mount Gerazim. It was the middle of the day, we were hot, tired and thirsty so

Jesus sent us into Sychar to buy food, whilst he stayed by the well. When we came back we were dumbfounded! We found our rabbi talking to a woman – a Samaritan woman! It is frowned upon for any man to talk to any woman in public and dishonouring for a rabbi to do so, but a Samaritan woman! Let me explain. Some 700 years before our Lord was born, the Assyrians invaded the northern kingdom of Israel. They took the inhabitants into exile and strangers were brought in to people the land, which from then on was known as Samaria. The Jews who were taken away seem to have disappeared from history and we call them the lost tribes. A hundred and fifty years later, Jerusalem was sacked by the Babylonians again and many more people were taken away, leaving only the poor and inadequate behind. Eventually our people were allowed back, but they were disheartened by what they found, and I don't only mean the condition of the Temple and the city. The inhabitants were no longer speaking Hebrew; they were now speaking Aramaic like their Samaritan neighbours (as we still do today). They had also intermarried and neglected the law of purity of our faith. The returned exiles were disgusted, banished them to Samaria and have had nothing to do with them since. It is not surprising that a rabbi would lose his reputation altogether if it were known that he had been talking to a Samaritan woman – and there we found Jesus doing just that! What they had been saying we didn't know until much later, but just as we arrived, she ran off into the town – leaving her water jar behind – and came back with friends, to introduce them to Jesus. They were all very impressed by what he had told her and asked that we should all stay with them and talk.

Jesus agreed, and we stayed for two days and many of them became convinced, and really believed that he was the Saviour of the World who was promised by the Jewish Prophets[3]. Jesus did not conform to standard protocol, and surprised us all many times after that incident, but he did succeed in spreading God's word in the most unexpected places.

We left Sychar and went on, via Nazareth to Cana and Capernaum. Jesus taught and healed many around that area, but he made his home in Capernaum on the shore of Galilee, when the people of Nazareth could not accept him. How could the son of their local carpenter, who had no rabbinical training, possibly 'set himself up as a Rabbi' and teach them anything? He had been born and bred in their town – they all knew his mother, brothers and sisters. How did he think he had miraculous powers? That did not stop him teaching and healing all around Galilee, nor from going up to Jerusalem for all the major festivals – and many others – and teaching in the Temple. The sick, the lame and the blind came from nearby and from far and wide to hear him and be healed – they believed! Even we, the chosen Twelve – although we recognised him as our special rabbi – did not appreciate who he was. He was Jesus – a man like us, with needs, feelings and emotions like ours – he was my cousin. Peter had called him 'The Christ', the 'Chosen One' – the 'One who was Expected'. We saw him feed a large crowd with next to nothing, we saw him walk on water, stop a storm with a simple rebuke, change water into

---

[3] The Samaritan 'Bible' contained only the first five books of our Bible. No Prophets, no Psalms, no Wisdom literature and none of the historical books.

wine, raise the dead and teach with such authority and confidence that he could have written the scriptures himself, but it was not until after he had died and risen that we really understood that he was the 'Son of God'! And we had spent three years in his company! Perhaps it is understandable that other people didn't accept him.

Jesus taught in public; he preached in the countryside and taught in the synagogues and in the Temple in Jerusalem. He offended the Jewish leaders and priests and often verbally attacked them. He accused them of not being true sons of Abraham, of having distorted the Law and of being blind to the will of God. Where the authorities were concerned, he never pulled his punches; he must have known from early in his ministry that they would reach breaking point and he would be put to death. He often talked of his cross; we thought that this was only a figure of speech, not that it really would be the end of him.

When we were in Jerusalem, we usually stayed in Bethany (a village some three or four milia outside Jerusalem, the other side of the Mount of Olives), with Martha, Mary and their brother Lazarus. They had a large house with outbuildings and could accommodate all of us together and we intended staying at their home just before the Passover when Jesus was killed. When we were approaching Judea on our way towards Jerusalem, a messenger met us on the way saying that Martha wanted Jesus to come urgently because Lazarus was desperately ill. Knowing how Jesus had healed many people in the past, we expected him to hurry to Bethany to be with Lazarus. Instead, we stopped at the tiny village we were in for another two days! We couldn't understand Jesus' delay. Jesus said Lazarus was 'asleep', although Martha seemed to think he was at death's door and when we reached Bethany, it seemed that she was right. He was dead and had been buried for four days. The women were desperately upset – justifiably, I thought – because Jesus had delayed on the way. They both said they believed that he could have healed him and prevented his death – if only he had arrived in time. I have rarely seen Jesus so upset as he was on that occasion. He openly wept! Whether for the loss of his friend or in sympathy with the sisters we didn't know, but he asked to be taken to the tomb. We all went – the family, friends and mourners and we, the Twelve. To our utter astonishment, Jesus asked for the great stone to be rolled back from the entrance of the tomb! No one wanted to be involved. They all said that after four days he would be decomposing and there would be a stench! Jesus insisted. Four men volunteered, picked up some poles for levers and set about it. After a while of sustained effort, the entrance was open, the stone chocked to prevent it rolling back and from where we were, all we could see was a black hole in the white rock. Jesus looked up to heaven, prayed aloud and called to Lazarus to come out. And he did! With some difficulty, because of the winding sheets, stiff with the spices used for the burial, but there he was! Jesus said, 'Loose him and let him go' and after being cut free, Lazarus walked down the hillside to join us. Now many of the Jews believe that the soul stays about the body for three days after death, but then leaves when decomposition sets in. This was the fourth day! Only God can restore life after such an interval.

Many of those in the mourning party believed in Jesus because of this and told everyone, when they went back to Jerusalem. Lazarus became famous for some time and Jesus got into even more contention with the chief priests and Pharisees because of it. They thought that if all the people were converted, Rome would take over and they would lose their position of authority – absolutely typical of that so-called 'pious' lot. They, therefore, plotted to kill both Jesus and Lazarus!

That was a busy week, though we didn't know that it was going to be the last week of Jesus' life. One particular thing – which still makes me feel uncomfortable, even all these years later – was Mother's visit to Bethany! She was at our town house, at the time, but came across to Bethany to see her favourite nephew – and us! I don't know whether Mother really understood at the time, what Jesus meant, when he talked of the Kingdom of God – his kingdom – but she had asked James and me, many times, what responsibilities we would have there. 'Ask him,' she had said to us, 'You're family. You can surely ask your cousin'. It wasn't something we could ask! We were part of his team; we were not trying to be more nor less than any of the others. On that occasion she managed to get Jesus and us cornered and said that if we weren't going to ask him, she would. She confronted him and asked to be granted a favour – she thought Jesus would do anything for his Auntie Sal. 'Allow my sons to sit one on either side of you, when you come into your Kingdom', she asked. He was rather taken aback and James and I could have crawled under the nearest stone, but he gently told her she didn't know what she was asking. He said that to grant such a request was for his Father, not him. He turned to us and asked us whether we thought we could take on his responsibilities. We did not need to answer. And how could either of us have coped with what he was to face later that week? The other ten were furious with us! How could we have allowed our mother to do such a thing? Who did we think we were, that such a privilege might be given to us? There was a lot of friction between us for a day or two, despite Jesus explaining to us that even he had come to serve and we must not seek greatness in that way. This was emphasised even more at our last Passover meal with him.

On the first day of the week, after we had arrived in Bethany, we went to Jerusalem. And how! We walked from Bethany to the eastern side of the Mount of Olives. There Jesus borrowed a donkey and her foal from a friend, threw his cloak over her back and rode from there up the hill. As we came along the road, over the brow of the hill, people going up to Jerusalem saw him. They cheered, shouted 'Hosanna!', tore down palm branches and strewed them in his path, and gave him a right royal welcome to the Holy City. We didn't realise, at the time, that Jesus was deliberately fulfilling Zechariah's prophecy and emphasising that he was the Anointed One. The crowds wouldn't let him go! He taught in the Temple courts and around and about in the city until late that evening, before going back to Bethany for a meal and rest.

As Passover approached, Jesus arranged to use the big room at the home of Mary, John Mark's mother, in Jerusalem, for our Passover meal – our last meal together before he was crucified, it transpired. Their home was near the palace of the high priest: our

Jerusalem house was towards the northern end of the city, near the Damascus Gate. It was a strange meal: all the usual trappings, but it was actually before Passover and Jesus seemed desperate to show us things he knew to be important, before the day was out. He knew – but we did not – that this was to be his last chance to do so before his death. During the meal I was reclining to his right and Judas was to his left – both of us in positions of honour! Then what embarrassment! Jesus got up, stripped to just a towel around his waist like the most lowly of servants (but at least he wasn't naked as many slaves are) and proceeded to do the most menial of servant's duties – he washed our feet! He said we must, similarly, be prepared to serve others and be humble. So much for Mother's request for us! Simon Peter protested vehemently! He wasn't going to let Jesus wash his feet! Jesus, in his gentle manner, said that if Peter wanted to be recognised as a member of his Kingdom, then he must accept what he was doing. Peter said if that was the case, he wanted to be washed all over, not just his feet. Typical! But none of us really understood what the implications of such service were, at that time.

Jesus dressed again, went back to the head of the table and went on to tell us that he would be betrayed, would die and would then go back to his Father and then send us the 'Holy Spirit'. Peter nudged me and said, 'Ask him what he means!' I couldn't! By this stage we were so confused – foot-washing, death, the 'Holy Spirit', the Comforter, betrayal – where could I start? At least, I thought I could ask him who could possibly betray him. Surely not one of us. Jesus simply said, 'It is the one to whom I shall give this piece of bread' and he gave it

to Judas! Judas immediately got up and went out –
we thought he was taking out funds for the poor;
how wrong could we be? If only we had realised at
the time we might have stopped him and changed
the horror of the next few days!

After the meal Jesus prayed long and beautiful
prayers – for us, the world and for himself and then
we went out into the dark, quiet city. We went past
the Pool of Siloam singing hymns, out through the
Ashpot Gate and along the Kidron valley beside the
city wall. Crossing over the Kidron brook, we made
for Gethsemane where Jesus often liked to go to pray.
It was part way up the side of the Mount of Olives,
overlooking the Temple. It was no wonder Jesus
liked it; it was a quiet olive grove, which provided the
peace and tranquillity he needed for prayer. That
night, it was particularly quiet; it was late, the city
was asleep, there wasn't even a breath of wind to
disturb the leaves on the trees. He left the other eight
of our company in the middle of the garden and took
Peter, James and me further up the hill. A bit higher
up was a flat rock where he always stood to pray and
he left the three of us below it, telling us to watch and
pray too. He went on, to his rock, but instead of
standing, as he usually did, he seemed to collapse –
first to his knees and then on all fours. He appeared
to be much more distressed than usual, during
prayer, but we couldn't hear what he was saying
because he was too far away. We three prayed, too,
for a while, but then we were tired and fell asleep.
He came back to us several times and woke us up,
remonstrating with us for not keeping watch – why
did we need to keep watch? We had been in that
garden to pray lots of times. It was as safe as
anywhere we knew, even if we stayed there all night.

The last time he woke us, we realised what he had been worried about! There were elders, priests, Temple guard and (it seemed) half the population of Jerusalem in that garden, with Judas leading them! He greeted Jesus and the guard instantly arrested him. We panicked and ran – anywhere away from that garden: up the hill, deeper into the trees and away to the roads beyond. I had run about two or three stadia and found Peter was just behind me. Peter was out of breath and stopped. I stopped, too. We listened, but could not hear anyone following. What were we to do? Where could we go? What had happened to Jesus? We were high enough to see the Temple and the Susa Gate, but all was quiet there. We tried to see the Kidron valley, but there were too many trees in the way, so we moved – cautiously – around the edge of Gethsemane, so that we could see the City Wall and the gate we had come through after supper. There were people there, with lights, just going through the gate: it had to be the arresting party and Jesus! Peter and I ran back down the hillside as fast as we could go, to get in through the gate before it was closed for the night – keeping well out of sight of the Temple guards and those with them. We got in without challenge and asked the guards at the gate what was happening. We were told that an arrest had been made and the prisoner was being taken to the high priest's palace for questioning. We thanked them and, trying not to look too suspicious, made our way to the palace, which was not far from the gate. But what now? The courtyard gate was shut. To find out what was happening we would, at least, have to get inside. I left Peter in the shadows and went to the gate. I knocked on it, my heart racing, and heard the bolts being drawn. As it creaked open, I saw – with relief – one of the high priest's servants whom I knew well from the times I had made the deliveries of fish to the palace. I told her I had seen all the activity and wondered what was going on. She told me that an arrest had been made and the prisoner was with the high priest, being questioned. There was a fire going, in the courtyard, and she invited me to join the other servants. I explained that I was with a friend and was told to bring him in too. Peter, in fear and trepidation, and in unfamiliar territory, came into the courtyard. As he came in, the servant-girl challenged Peter with being a disciple of the prisoner, but he denied it. I left him at the fireside and went into the palace with one of the other girls, who took me into the hall where Jesus was being questioned. We stood in the shadows, behind a pillar, so that we would not be seen, but would be able to hear what was going on. Annas, the priest whose daughter was married to Caiaphas (who was the high priest that year), was questioning Jesus about his teaching and Jesus upset him by saying if he really wanted to know, he should ask the people in the Temple and the synagogues who would know what he had taught them. Annas sent him off, under guard, to Caiaphas and I returned to the courtyard. As I came back, Peter was arguing with another of the servants, who also thought he was a disciple. Later, the brother of the high priest's servant Malchus (whose ear Peter had cut off when Jesus was arrested) said he was sure he had seen Peter in Gethsemane. At this, Peter really lost his temper and cursed and swore that he did not know Jesus. Just at that moment, the cock crowed and Jesus was brought out into the courtyard, on the way to the Antonia fortress – Pilate's residence. He just looked at Peter! Peter didn't know what to do. He stumbled out of the courtyard with tears running down his face.

What should I do now? Should I go after Peter? Would the high priest's staff challenge me, as they had Peter, if I did so? How would I know what was happening to Jesus, if I didn't stay in touch with the palace staff? I stayed, but I lost track of Peter for the next couple of days.

The palace grape-vine worked amazingly well. That little collection of servants was kept informed of Jesus' journeys to Pilate's judgement hall, from Pilate to Herod and back again. They knew all that had been said. They knew that the chief priests wanted Jesus dead, and of Pilate's plan to offer the release of a prisoner at Passover – it was an old custom. Would the people have Jesus BarAbbas[4] – a convicted zealot, or Jesus BarJoseph[5] – the 'King of the Jews'? The invitation to the populace was to be made at the stone pavement (Gabbatha, in Aramaic) in front of the judgement hall at the Antonia Fortress at daybreak. When I learned this, I went as fast as I could to our town-house; Aunt Mary was staying with Mother for the Passover and neither of them knew that Jesus had even been arrested!

When I got in, Mother came to find out where I had been and why I was coming in at such an hour; it doesn't matter how old you are, mothers always think of their sons as children. She was devastated when she heard my news. Her nephew at such risk! And what had happened to James? Where was he? I

---

[4] Son of Abbas

[5] Son of Joseph

sat her down with a goblet of wine and told her all I knew. James had got away from Gethsemane, as Peter and I had, but I didn't know where he was. I was fairly certain that he would be alright, since no one had mentioned him. But what were we going to do about Aunt Mary? It was not long to dawn, by this time, so we agreed that I would go to the pavement at daybreak, find out what the verdict would be and report back as quickly as possible. There was little point in waking Aunt Mary before we knew what was to happen. If she woke before I returned, Mother would tell her all that had occurred and what we knew so far.

There was already a crowd at the pavement when I got there and by the time Pilate appeared there were hundreds. Some of the faces I recognised; they had cheered when Jesus had ridden into the Temple a week earlier. Now many of them seemed to be angry and anxious for Jesus' death! When Pilate came out, they started shouting, encouraged by the priests to demand crucifixion for Jesus. They quietened a little, when Pilate sat down, but as soon as the two prisoners were brought out for the release offer to be made, they started up again. They were uncontrollable: they wanted BarAbbas released and Jesus dead! Despite all Pilate said to them, he could see he was going to have a riot on his hands, if he wasn't careful. He couldn't let that happen. He knew there would be trouble with Caesar, if it did, and he could not run that risk. It was obviously against his better judgement, but he let BarAbbas go and sent Jesus to the cross. After washing his hands, he went back in to the judgement hall. I knew what was to happen next; Jesus would have to carry the crossbar of his cross through the streets to Golgotha, be nailed to it and left to die, with a Roman guard keeping watch. I was shattered! My cousin, my innocent Master, was to die an agonising, criminal's death, for what? All this because he had exposed the hypocrisy of the Jewish establishment and their authority had been challenged! I pushed my way through the crowd, unable to see clearly through tear-wet eyes, and went back home. What could we say to Aunt Mary now?

When I got in, I found Mother quietly consoling Aunt Mary, but then had to break the horrific news of what was to follow next. They were both distraught. I tried to persuade them to stay at home whilst I should go to Golgotha, but they wouldn't have it. They would both come too! I knew how long it would take the guards to get Jesus there and how long the preliminaries would take, so I made sure that enough time elapsed before I got my Mother and Aunt to the site of execution. When we reached Golgotha, we found three crucifixes, with Jesus, naked, on the central one. I have never had such a harrowing experience – neither before nor since. Aunt Mary must have been going through 'the valley of the shadow of death'!

Soon after we got there, Mary of Magdala, and Aunt Mary's cousin Mary, who was married to Clopas, joined us. Apart from simply being there, there is absolutely nothing one can do to help. Nothing one can say: nothing one can do. Utterly helpless! To add insult to injury, the Roman execution party were doing what the law permitted – casting lots for his clothing. They were not even interested in the torture above them. Jesus was, initially, distracted with pain and did not know we were there. When he saw us, he told me to accept his mother like my mother, and her to accept me as her son. Aunt Mary virtually collapsed with this emotional strain and I told Mother I would take her home. Mother came too and after we had got home, given Aunt Mary wine with a few drops of tincture of mandrake[6] in it to calm her, I left Mother to comfort her and went back to Golgotha.

By the time I had returned to the crosses, it was about the sixth hour[7] and soon after – inexplicably – the daylight gradually disappeared. It became twilight in the middle of the day! How could the sun have disappeared? There was a general feeling of apprehension amongst the guard and those standing near. No one knew what was happening! There was a sinister atmosphere about that hill for the next few hours and little was said by anyone. About the ninth hour, Jesus spoke. He said he was thirsty. One of the guards dipped a sponge in wine vinegar, put it on a dhura[8] cane and gave it to him to drink. When he had swallowed some of it, he said, 'It is accomplished', gave up his spirit and died.

The day was wearing on. At the twelfth hour the Sabbath would begin – and this Sabbath was Passover – and it was not acceptable for bodies to be left hanging on crosses on the Sabbath. The Jews asked

---

[6] Mandrake (Mandragora) grows naturally around the Mediterranean and its active constituent can be extracted with alcohol. (See footnote 3, page 95.)

[7] Time was calculated from 0600 hours, so the sixth hour would be 1200 hours (mid-day).

[8] The dhura cane – or stem of the hyssop – is strong and straight and may be up to two metres in length. It is otherwise known as Jerusalem corn and was a main and nutritious part of the local diet.

that their legs should be broken, so that they would die more quickly. The soldiers agreed to do so, but when they came to Jesus, they found that he was dead already. Just to ensure it – because he had been offered 'morion'[9] whilst he was on the cross – the centurion in charge of the execution party followed routine orders and stuck a spear into his side; a gush of blood and water came out. I stood there, watching, totally incapable of taking my eyes off the horrible sight. Jesus made no movement. The spear thrust was well aimed: he was dead. The centurion was experienced and he certainly had no doubts! As the bodies were being taken down, Joseph of Arimathea went to ask Pilate for permission to take Jesus' body for burial, otherwise it would just have been left for the animals to devour on Gehenna, the rubbish tip to the south of the city wall. Pilate agreed and from a distance, I watched Joseph, together with Nicodemus, take the body, wrap it in linen with about 100 litrai[10] of myrrh and aloes, and lay it in a new tomb in Joseph's garden nearby. They then closed the tomb with the huge round stone, which rolled across its entrance. They were both elderly and they had a lot of difficulty with it, even though it was to roll downhill in the specially constructed channel. It was just before sunset – before the beginning of the Sabbath – that all was completed, and I went back home to Mother and Aunt Mary.

---

[9] (See footnote 6 above and footnote 3 in Luke) Roman standing orders for the execution guard required that death be confirmed with a well-aimed spear thrust up into the heart through the left side, if morion had been offered to any crucified criminal.

[10] About 34 kilograms in total.

It was quite the worst Passover that any of my family has ever known. We observed the rituals, but it was impossible to eat anything. Aunt Mary was inconsolable, constantly in tears and desolated that she had not been with him at his death, nor had she been able to prepare his body for burial. We told her that she could, no doubt, visit the grave on the first day of the week – after Passover – as long as we had permission from Joseph and it was very unlikely that he would refuse her. She got no sleep that night. We tried to keep her calm with some wine with tincture of mandrake as best we could, but there was little else I could do. Since I had learned that some of the Twelve had found their way back to John Mark's mother's home, early the next morning I left Mother to cope and went around to see them – even though it was significantly further than the statutory Sabbath Day's Journey of 2000 cubits[11]!

There were few people about and I got to the house easily, without being challenged by anyone. I slipped into their courtyard, up the steps to the upper room and knocked on the door – we had a coded knock, but the door was opened very cautiously. I cannot tell you the relief of finding my brother James there! Peter was there too, with his brother Andrew. He was withdrawn, depressed and uncommunicative; Andrew was trying to cheer him up – without a great deal of success. We talked for a while. John Mark brought us some wine, fruit, bread and cheese, but we had little appetite. Somewhere about the twelfth

---

[11] A cubit is the distance between the bend in the elbow and the finger tips: about 18 inches or 45 centimetres. A Sabbath day's journey was therefore about 1,000 yards or 900 metres.

hour I left them and went back to Mother and Aunt Mary, telling them I would return later, but to call me earlier, if need be. I felt that I had to support Aunt Mary, but in a situation of illness or distress, women are much better at coping than men are. All I could do was to lend moral support! I busied myself with things that needed doing about the house, with things relating to our fishing business and simply being available. Mother needed sleep, so I sat with Aunt Mary – who just couldn't rest. She cried, she talked, she reminisced, she worried! Eventually, she lapsed into fitful sleep and I dozed off.

Very early the next morning, long before first light, Mother woke me; she was worried about James, so would I go to ensure he was safe! Yes Mother! Of course, Mother! Of course he would be safe – but I went back to check. As I was approaching the house, I saw someone in the shadows – my heart raced – but it was Judas, James' son! We went to join the others together and all of them, except for Thomas, had found their way back. We had not been there long when there was the sound of many running feet outside and soon after that, Mary of Magdala came banging on the door, demanding that we let her in. She told us the tomb was empty and she had seen Jesus! The guard at the tomb had gone and she had seen an angel there! Peter looked at me: I looked at him and we obviously thought the same thing – hysterical women – but we'd better go and check. We crept out quietly, but once in the street we began to run in the direction of Joseph's garden. I could run faster than Peter and I got there first. There were no guards in sight. There was nobody about. All was still and quiet. The tomb gaped open. The huge closing stone seemed to have been thrown from the

entrance and was lying some distance away. I looked
in and there was no body there – the grave clothes
were lying where the body should have been, with
the head-cloth separate from them. Peter caught up
and went into the tomb – Jesus had simply
disappeared, seemingly straight through the burial
wrappings! We looked at each other dumbfounded!
Was this what Jesus meant when he said he would
rise again? We walked back pensively to rejoin the
others and tell them that Mary was right! We didn't
say much to each other on the way; I suppose we
were too confused to put anything into words, but
when we got back, we tried to explain all we had seen
(or not seen) to the others, who were still arguing
with Mary in the big room. They didn't believe us
any more than we had believed Mary! Later that
evening we were back in the same place again; it had
a feeling of safety and reassurance. We were talking
about what had happened earlier that morning, but
then we heard a familiar voice. We turned as one,
towards the sound and there was Jesus! 'Peace be
with you!' he said again and then talked to us in the
old, familiar way. He told us we would receive the
Holy Spirit and we would be given the power to
forgive sins – and then he was gone. He just
disappeared! He didn't go out through the door: he
just wasn't there anymore. Thomas came in a bit
later and we excitedly tried to tell him that we had
seen Jesus: Thomas was always a bit sceptical, but
this was too much for him to accept! He said he
would have to see the marks of crucifixion before he
would believe us – we must have imagined it or seen
someone else.

It was about a week later that we all met up again
in Mary's big room and Thomas was with us this

time. The door was locked for safety and we were again discussing all that had occurred in the past ten days or so. Again we heard the familiar voice say 'Peace be with you!' and there was Jesus standing against the wall opposite the door! He immediately called Thomas to touch his wounds, as though he knew what Thomas had said to us. Thomas was dumbfounded! He dropped to his knees saying, 'My Lord and my God!' Jesus told us that many would be blessed because they would believe, even though they had not actually seen him as we had. Again, whilst we were talking, he was suddenly not there!

We saw him many times over the course of about six weeks from the time he came back from the dead – once he was cooking fish on the beach when we returned from fishing. That time I remember particularly, because after we had finished eating, Peter got quite upset with him. Jesus asked Peter three times whether he loved him and each time after Peter answered, he told him to look after his followers. I think it might have been his way of cancelling the three times Peter denied knowing him, that night in the High Priest's courtyard, after he had been arrested. It was at Pentecost – about a week after we last saw Jesus – that everything changed. We seemed to be fired with enthusiasm and fearlessness. Jesus had told us he would send us someone like him, called the Holy Spirit – and he did. We preached and taught in the city and in the Temple. A favourite place was Solomon's colonnade on the eastern side of the Temple where Jesus had liked to walk and teach: Peter and I frequently went there together. In fact, we were together quite a lot and we began to find that the new believers – and the other disciples – expected us to organise and be responsible for all Jesus' followers. That was all very well, but the combination of teaching as Jesus had done and being recognised as the leaders of Jesus' followers led us into terrible trouble with the authorities and on several occasions we were arrested, imprisoned and threatened with beating. Many times I recalled Jesus' face when he had asked James and me – in front of Mother and the others – whether we thought we could 'drink of the cup he had to drink from'! But it was not all threat: often it was exciting and fun! On one occasion Peter and I went to Samaria. The brothers had heard that Philip had been teaching in Samaria and many, many people had accepted the Word. We were despatched to find out whether this was true and what had happened. We were amazed! Philip had worked hard. Even Simon the Sorcerer said he was converted. We stayed a while and then returned, teaching and preaching on the way, being supported by many believers in the small villages on the way.

As time went on, we began to travel and teach separately, meeting up in Jerusalem fairly often to exchange views on the progress of The Way, as our new faith was coming to be known. There were many converts in Syria and Asia Minor, but progress of the faith in and around Jerusalem and Judea, amongst the Jews, where my brother James taught, was very slow. We met enormous resistance and antagonism. As much as James had tried, most refused to accept that Jesus was the divine Son of God. Jesus' brother James – by then a firm believer – took on the responsibility for the church in Jerusalem, Peter travelled eastward towards Babylon and I taught around Galilee and travelled more towards the North and Asia Minor. Despite Jesus' dying request,

I could not take Aunt Mary with me when travelling, so she stayed with Mother in our home at Capernaum and I went back as often as I could to see them both. I was never away for long, at that time, and when I was, my brother James kept an eye on them, but some fifteen years or so after Jesus died, Herod arrested him and had him beheaded! I stayed nearer home for a long time, after that. Mother seemed to cope fairly well, following James' death, but I thought I should take the opportunity to be closer to her and Aunt Mary and stay and teach where my brother had taught, to see if I could impress on our Jewish brothers who Jesus was and what he had come to do and give to us all. I knew that I would have a struggle to gain converts – quite apart from avoiding even more trouble with the authorities. Ten years went by, almost without noticing them! Teaching, preaching, the administration of the new church – together with a bit of fishing and supervising the business – all kept me fully occupied. During this time, our new brother Paul had been travelling, teaching and setting up new churches in Asia Minor, Achaia and Macedonia, but then he was put under house arrest in Caesarea after a disturbance in Jerusalem. Young Timothy had been left caring for the churches in Asia Minor, but he needed someone more senior for support. Knowing the area, I left Mother and Aunt Mary again and went to Ephesus to see what I could offer. Ephesus is a stunningly beautiful city! Everywhere you look, there is gleaming white marble. Some has been defaced by paintwork, but the workmanship put into the carving of the pillars and capitals, the way the stone is cut – so precisely that each fits perfectly on or against its neighbour – is of high quality. And the Harbour Street is unbelievable! It is a colonnaded, marble roadway, running from the grand theatre, straight down to the harbour. The seafarer's first sight of the city is breath-taking! A marble road runs to the right, just in front of the theatre, and adjacent to this is the commercial agora – almost the busiest place in the city. Many tradesmen and artisans worked there: silversmiths made miniature shrines of Artemis and sold them there. Ephesus was the home of her idol; there is a great Temple to her and Ephesus is virtually ruled by her. It was there, and because of her, that our brother Paul ran into trouble and caused a riot!

The church at Ephesus was strong – Paul had worked well! They accepted me as an Elder and I made Ephesus my base for supervising the entire area. Once I had established a home, I returned to Capernaum to see Mother and Aunt Mary and to settle family business. I dared to suggest that she and Aunt Mary should come back to Asia Minor with me. Mother flatly refused! Aunt Mary could do so if she wished, but she could manage perfectly well in her own home, thank you very much! She said she had plenty to occupy her, quite apart from still needing to supervise the fishing business, so she was not going anywhere. When she has made up her mind, Mother will not be deterred. She was financially secure and I was sure that she would cope on her own, so I took Aunt Mary with me, back to Ephesus.

It must have been a somewhat daunting prospect for the old lady: travelling overland would not have been easy for her, so we went to Caesarea where we found a Roman grain ship going to Patara. From there we were fortunate in finding another vessel plying the coastal towns of Asia Minor, which would take us to Ephesus. Although her accommodation aboard each of the ships was comfortable, Aunt Mary was glad to reach my new home and settle in.

It is such a long time ago! Aunt Mary seemed to enjoy living at Ephesus and was pleased to be involved with our church. Most of the members of our church here are Greeks and they considered it an honour to talk to the Hebrew lady who was the mother of our Lord! Sadly, she died a few years after coming to Ephesus. It is such a pity that so few of the Jews here are prepared to accept Jesus as Lord. Perhaps Roman persecution has been a factor. The Emperor Domitian didn't like us. He thought he was 'god' and demanded that the entire world pay homage to him as such – and threatened death to those who didn't. Few outside Rome were killed, but he made life very difficult for us and I was banished to Patmos for a few years for refusing to renounce my faith. It was not easy – I was no longer a young man and was forced into hard labour on that remote and isolated, rocky island, but it did give me time for thought. The Lord also appeared to me there: another appearance and to me, personally, so long after his death and ascension! He blessed me with a sight of heaven and gave me letters for the seven churches in Asia Minor. I was given a foretaste of the latter days of the world – and I had time to write it all down! My problem was that I had to write it myself. I am a fisherman, not a learned scholar. I can speak and write Greek, but my hand is slow and not very efficient. My disciple, John the Elder, is much better at writing than I. However, despite all my difficulties, my report of the Apocalypse to come has been read all around Asia Minor, as well as in our Church here at Ephesus. I am told that, as a result, the brothers, who are mostly Greeks, now understand that the future belongs to the Lord alone and that my allusions to the Hebrew scriptures, and to the Book of Daniel in particular, convey this information in a way that they find easy to accept.

Well, my Apocalyptic treatise was written a long time ago, but it seems as though I have been writing ever since! The elders, brothers, many of my friends and even my young disciple Polycarp (I'm sure he will be a powerful voice for our Faith in the future) have insisted that since Mark, Matthew and Luke have written about Jesus' life and teaching, I should write too, but with more of a spiritual bias than the historical way the others have done. My disciple, John – I've told you about John, haven't I? – he has been a great encouragement to me with this, and wrote beautifully at my dictation. He is a good amanuensis. I cannot see well now and it would not have been possible to have done it all myself, but with his help it has been achieved. It is as much as I can do now to cope with being carried about to attend meetings and to advise the brothers. There have been many false prophets in Ephesus! Deceivers and antichrists who even deny that Jesus was human like us. How can they say he was the Expected One if he was not a man, born like us? They claim to know God and abide in him, but they live unrighteous and uncharitable lives! John persuaded me to write a letter to the churches, expanding some of the points I made in my writings about Jesus, to challenge these heresies. He wanted me to write another letter or two, but I am too tired and old, now, so I have suggested what format such letters should take and some points he should include, but he will have to write them himself. I may endorse them, but I must step back and let the younger ones take over now. My time is running out. I must rest again – so tired – even doing nothing! Soon I shall be with Jesus and the Father and The Way will be in the hands of the new believers. I must go. God bless you all, little children – and don't forget to love one another!

References and Sources

Atlas of Bible Times – Lion Publishing

BST(The Bible Speaks Today):
>Mark – Donald English
>Luke – Michael Wilcock
>John – Bruce Milne
>Acts – J.R.W.Stott

The Daily Study Bible:
>Matthew – William Barclay
>Mark – William Barclay
>Luke – William Barclay
>John – William Barclay

IVP Commentaries:
>Mark – R. Alan Cole
>Matthew – R.T.France
>Luke – Leon Morris
>John – R.V.G.Tasker
>Acts – I.Howard Marshall
>Acts – E.M.Blaiklock – Tyndale Press

The Holy Bible – New International Version (Thompson's Chain)

The Illustrated Bible Dictionaries – IVP

The Student Bible Atlas – Dr Tim Dowley – Kingsway Publications

Collins map of Israel (featuring Bartholomew mapping) – 1998

Insight Travel Map – Turkey West

Cruden's Complete Concordance to the Old and New
    Testaments – Lutterworth

Dictionary of Jesus and the Gospels – IVP Joel B.
    Green, Scot McKnight, & I. Howard Marshall
The Lion Handbook to the Bible

People Just Like Us
            – J.Oswald Sanders – Bridge Publishing
The Master's Men
            – William Barclay – SCM Press Ltd.
Mary the Mother of Jesus
            – Wendy Virgo – Kingsway Publications
Men and Women of the New Testament
            – Derek Thomas – Autumn House
The Book of Witnesses
            – David Kossoff – Collins

PC Study Bible for Windows – Biblesoft
Encarta 97 – Microsoft

The Heavenly Debate
            – Mick Brown – Daily Telegraph 19.12.1998
The Son of God – BBC Television April 2001

Narcosis and Nightshade. A.J.Carter B.M.J 1996; 313:
    1630-1632
All the Plants of the Bible. Winifred Walker –
    Lutterworth Press.

Personal communication
            – Dr David Price Williams BA., PhD., FRGS
            – Mr J. Richard Collin MA., FRCS., DO